MENTAL HEALTH REHABILITATION: DISPUTING IRRATIONAL BELIEFS

ABOUT THE AUTHOR

GERALD L. GANDY, Ph.D., CRC, NCC: Professor of Rehabilitation Counseling, School of Allied Health Professions, Medical College of Virginia, Virginia Commonwealth University, Richmond, Virginia. Formerly, President of the Faculty, School of Community and Public Affairs and Director, Rehabilitation Services Education Program, Virginia Commonwealth University; Chief, Counseling and Rehabilitation Services, Veterans Administration Regional Office, Columbia, South Carolina; Counselor, University of South Carolina Counseling Center; and Captain, United States Army Medical Services Corps. Including this book, Doctor Gandy has either authored or co-authored/co-edited four major textbooks and contributed numerous articles to the professional literature. Doctor Gandy has been active in local, national, and international professional association activities. For example, he received an award for "Special Recognition for School and University Leadership" at Virginia Commonwealth University, chaired a National Committee on Rehabilitation Services Education, and has made numerous presentations at national and international conferences. Doctor Gandy is a Licensed Professional Counselor (Virginia) and a Licensed Psychologist (South Carolina). He is certified by the Commission on Rehabilitation Counselor Certification and the National Board for Certified Counselors and is registered with the National Register of Health Service Providers in Psychology. Doctor Gandy is also a Fellow and Diplomate in Professional Counseling of the International Academy of Behavioral Medicine, Counseling and Psychotherapy.

MENTAL HEALTH REHABILITATION: DISPUTING IRRATIONAL BELIEFS

By

GERALD L. GANDY, Ph.D., CRC, NCC

Professor of Rehabilitation Counseling
School of Allied Health Professions
Medical College of Virginia
Virginia Commonwealth University
Richmond, Virginia

With a Foreword by

ALBERT ELLIS, Ph.D.

President
Institute for Rational-Emotive Therapy
New York, New York

CHARLES C THOMAS • PUBLISHER
Springfield • Illinois • U.S.A.

Published and Distributed Throughout the World by

CHARLES C THOMAS • PUBLISHER
2600 South First Street
Springfield, Illinois 62794-9265

© *1995 by* CHARLES C THOMAS • PUBLISHER

ISBN 0-398-06531-4   (cloth)
ISBN 0-398-06532-2   (paper)

Library of Congress Catalog Card Number: 95-16978

Printed in the United States of America
SC-R-3

Library of Congress Cataloging-in-Publication Data

Gandy, Gerald L.
    Mental Health rehabilitation : disputing irrational beliefs / by
Gerald L. Gandy.
        p.   cm.
    Includes bibliographical references and index.
    ISBN 0-398-06531-4 (cloth). — ISBN 0-398-06532-2 (pbk.)
    1. Mentally ill—Rehabilitation.   2. Physically handicapped—
Rehabilitation.   I. Title.
RC439.5.G36   1995
362.2'0425—dc20   95-16978
                                                                    CIP

For my Beloved Wife, Patricia Haltiwanger Gandy.
PATRICIA, who makes the ideal of
compatibility a reality for me.

FOREWORD

If anyone is equipped to write a book on the use of Rational Emotive Behavior Therapy (REBT) in Mental Health Rehabilitation, it is certainly Gerald Gandy. He is a full professor of rehabilitation counseling at a leading medical college and university, and he has previously published a number of outstanding papers and books in this important area. He is also well trained in REBT; and by supervising some of his work and keeping in close touch with him during the last decade, I have found that his counseling, his talks, and his writings on it are highly well-informed and accurate. If I were to select anyone in the world to write an authoritative and comprehensive book on REBT counseling and psychotherapy applied to people with rehabilitation problems, it would definitely be Dr. Gandy. So I am delighted with his choosing to do this book and think that he has carried it off remarkably well.

As Dr. Gandy points out, Rational Emotive Behavior Therapy has always been designed to help a multiversity of individuals, including those with severe physical, mental, and emotional handicaps and disorders. How? By teaching all individuals who will listen—clients, readers, students, and professionals—two important philosophies:

First, they can always give themselves unconditional self-acceptance (USA), just because they are alive and human, just because they decide to fully accept themselves; Yes, *whether or not* they perform well and *whether or not* other people love or approve of them.

Second, REBT shows people that nothing—no, nothing—is "awful," "horrible," and "terrible," even when it is very frustrating and difficult to manage.

If people with virtually *any* kind of problem or disadvantage will acquire—and *really* believe in—these two core philosophies, they will still often be, for physical and environmental reasons, sorely put upon and handicapped. But they will not be self-deprecating and not make themselves a victim of their own demandingness and consequent low frustration tolerance.

These lessons are among the many REBT ideas that Gerald Gandy clearly, accurately, and persuasively presents in this book. His writing is particularly good as he emphasizes how different people's dysfunctional, irrational beliefs can be actively disputed and can be experimentally and behaviorally worked against. He covers the REBT approach to several of the most important physical and mental disturbances. His Chapter 7, "Personality Disorder," is especially valuable, as it shows how, in the case of an arrant, arrogant narcissist, the therapist's teaching him how to discover, dispute, and strongly act against his grandiose, self-defeating beliefs worked remarkably well—even with this individual who was more than neurotic and who had a severe personality disorder.

Gerald Gandy's book will not make any counselor or therapist perfect and will not show him or her how to completely cure everyone with a serious rehabilitation problem. But it is an unusual book for anyone concerned with mental and emotional rehabilitation, and it will, I predict, prove to be highly influential and useful in this important mental health area.

Albert Ellis, Ph.D., President
Institute for Rational-Emotive Therapy
45 East 65th Street
New York, NY 10021-6593

PREFACE

This textbook is based on the pioneering work of Dr. Albert Ellis, a clinical psychologist, who combined humanistic, philosophical, and behavioral therapy to develop Rational Emotive Behavior Therapy (REBT). Doctor Ellis was originally trained as a classical psychoanalyst but deviated from this background to initiate the cognitive-behavioral revolution in psychotherapy. Cognitive-behavioral techniques are now considered by most researchers to be among the most efficient and effective techniques in counseling and psychotherapy. Cognitive-behavior therapies utilize cognitive, emotive, and behavioral techniques to change attitudes and beliefs in a manner that will have a constructive impact on emotions and behavior.

Although Dr. Albert Ellis has always employed a variety of cognitive, emotive, and behavioral techniques, this textbook will focus on what originally made his approach radically different from other psychotherapeutic orientations—his contribution of rational restructuring or the disputing of irrational beliefs. The disputing of irrational beliefs and their relationship to emotional and behavioral change will be illustrated in a systematic written homework (SWH) framework. The SWH format, adapted from the work of Dr. Albert Ellis and others, is a writing assignment in which a person is given instructions regarding the application of the principles of REBT to his or her emotional problems.

The disputing of irrational beliefs within the SWH format will be applied to case examples of the mental health rehabilitation of individuals with mental and physical disabilities. Mental health rehabilitation is defined as therapeutic counseling designed to facilitate the emotional development of individuals with mental and physical disabilities that enables them to lead more productive lives. Productivity is considered to include avocational as well as vocational activities. The terms counseling and therapy are used interchangeably.

This textbook should be applicable to a wide variety of disciplines involved with therapeutic counseling of people with mental and/or physical disabilities such as rehabilitation counseling, mental health counseling, pastoral counseling, school counseling, clinical social work, clinical and counseling psychology, and behavioral science oriented medical specialties (e.g., psychiatry, physiatry, and occupational medicine) and related health professions (e.g., behavioral optometry, psychiatric nursing, recreational therapy, occupational therapy, and physical therapy). Readers are encouraged to conceptualize the cases in terms of their own discipline and how they might incorporate the disputing of irrational beliefs into their own therapeutic orientation.

Therefore, the textbook should serve as an ideal resource guide for a variety of mental health practitioners. It could serve as the primary reading source for short-term community workshops or institutional in-service training programs. The book would also be a useful secondary companion reference in graduate courses in the various mental health disciplines.

"Part One: Introduction" includes the first three chapters. The first chapter provides a brief overview of the basic principles of REBT. The second chapter describes and discusses the application of REBT to mental health rehabilitation. The third chapter explains and provides guidelines for the disputing irrational beliefs within the SWH format. The first three chapters are an extensive expansion that is based in part on an article entitled "Disputing Irrational Beliefs in Rehabilitation Counseling" that I published in the *Journal of Applied Rehabilitation Counseling, 26*(1), 36–40, 1995. The journal publication was based on a presentation with the same title that I made at the Fourth International Conference on Stress Management in Paris, France, on September 4, 1992.

"Part Two: Case Studies" includes six chapters that provide case illustrations representing deafness, mood disorder, blindness, personality disorder, spinal cord injury, and substance abuse. They represent a small sample of all possible disabilities, but the purpose is to illustrate the disputing of irrational beliefs in the SWH format with representative major mental and physical disabilities. Although the cases are composites of various individuals, they are based on my experiences for the past twenty-five years in working with people with disabilities. The cases are also presented to emphasize the holistic nature of people with disabilities and include educational, vocational, and avocational aspects as well as personal and social concerns.

My background is that of a rehabilitation counselor educator who, since 1975, has had a specific academic interest in adapting REBT concepts and techniques to the discipline of rehabilitation counseling. I have taught an advanced graduate counseling course that focuses on the application of REBT to rehabilitation counseling since 1978. My interest in cognitive-behavioral techniques and, more specifically, REBT emerged between 1970 and 1975 when I was a counseling psychologist with the Veterans Administration Vocational Rehabilitation Program. I consider myself very fortunate to have had the opportunity to study with Dr. Albert Ellis by attendance at workshops at his Institute for Rational-Emotive Therapy in New York City and in other locations and through sending him audiotapes and videotapes over the years. He has been more than generous in my consultations with him and in encouraging me in my combination of REBT with rehabilitation counseling.

Special recognition and appreciation is extended to Dr. Richard E. Hardy, Professor and Chair, Department of Rehabilitation Counseling, who reviewed my proposal and recommended it to the publisher, as well as for his comments on the book. Special appreciation is extended to Dr. E. Davis Martin, Jr. and Dr. Warren R. Rule, Professors of Rehabilitation Counseling, for reviewing my proposal as well as commenting on part of the book. Special appreciation is also extended to all of my other colleagues and professors in the Department of Rehabilitation Counseling at Virginia Commonwealth University for their support as well as their comments on various parts of this book: Dr. Anne L. Chandler, Dr. Marcia J. Lawton, Dr. Richard S. Luck, and Mr. William McDowell.

Special thanks is extended to Dr. Robert A. Lassiter, Professor Emeritus, and Dr. Martha H. Lassiter, former Adjunct Professor, for their comments on part of the book. Dr. Robert A. Lassiter, an Associate Fellow recipient of the New York Institute for Rational-Emotive Therapy, also reviewed my proposal and has been very influential in the development of my interest in REBT. Thanks also to Dr. George R. Jarrell and Mr. Keith C. Wright, Professor Emeriti, for their prior general influence as colleagues and to Ms. Mary Tucker, our Departmental Secretary, for her technical advice and constant encouragement.

A special tribute of gratitude is extended to my wife, Patricia, to whom this book is dedicated — a management analyst and highly talented professional in her own right, not only for her expert editorial assistance and insights, but also for her enduring love and patience.

G.L.G.

CONTENTS

MENTAL HEALTH REHABILITATION: DISPUTING IRRATIONAL BELIEFS

Part One
INTRODUCTION

Chapter 1

OVERVIEW OF RATIONAL EMOTIVE BEHAVIOR THERAPY (REBT)

Albert Ellis (1994) has practiced psychotherapy, marriage and family counseling, as well as sex therapy, for over fifty years and continues this practice at the Institute for Rational-Emotive Therapy in New York City. He also continues to give lectures and conduct workshops not only in the United States but in numerous foreign countries. Originally trained as a classical psychoanalyst, he deviated from this background and began to develop Rational Emotive Behavior Therapy (REBT) in January, 1955. He has now authored or edited over fifty books and six hundred articles. His contributions led to the cognitive-behavioral revolution in psychotherapy and have spread REBT throughout the world. The purpose of this chapter is to provide a brief overview of the REBT model with suggestions for further study.

BASIC CONCEPTS

A basic philosophical premise of REBT is that, at least in Western society, people want to be happy (Ellis, 1962, 1973, 1994). The extent to which people achieve their own individualized goals of happiness is greatly influenced by engaging in rational behavior and avoiding irrational behavior. The basic definition of rational in REBT theory "means that which helps people to achieve their basic goals and purposes, whereas irrational means that which prevents them from achieving these goals and purposes" (Ellis & Dryden, 1987, p. 4). The definition of rational utilized is based on the principles of the scientific method (Ellis & Harper, 1975).

An important concept in REBT is unconditional self-acceptance (Ellis & Dryden, 1987; Wessler & Wessler, 1980). Healthy people are glad to be alive and accept themselves just because they are alive. They do not measure their intrinsic worth by their extrinsic achievements or by what others think of them. They avoid rating themselves—their totality or their being (Hauck, 1992). They avoid unconstructive guilt or blame, either of one's self or others (Ard, 1990). REBT also places a focus on constructive self-interest (Ellis & Dryden, 1987). Constructive self-interest demands social interest in order for an individual to help build the kind of society in which one would best live oneself.

REBT theory hypothesizes that humans have a biological tendency to think irrationally but also have a biological tendency to think rationally (Ellis & Dryden, 1987; Ellis & Grieger, 1986). The biological tendency to think irrationally is based on the seeming ease with which humans think crookedly and the prevalence of such thinking, even among people who have been rationally raised. However, REBT theory holds that humans also have a biological tendency to exercise the power of human choice and to work toward changing their irrational thinking.

When people become emotionally upset about an event, REBT postulates that their emotional reaction is caused more by their interpretation of the event rather than by the actual event itself (Ellis & Bernard, 1986). If they are rejected for a job, they may get depressed; They assume the rejection caused the depression. However, they probably silently verbalized to themselves that the event should not have happened and they are failures for being rejected. These ideas are highly irrational since there is no reason why they should not be rejected for the job, and there is no evidence why they will not have an opportunity to be successful in the future. More rational ideas could be that they wish the event had not happened and they do not like failing. These ideas would probably cause them to only feel annoyed and frustrated but remain determined to try again.

A distinction is made between inappropriate or disturbed emotions (anger, shame, anxiety, depression, etc.) and appropriate or nondisturbed emotions (displeasure, regret, concern, sadness, etc.) in REBT (Ellis & Bernard, 1986; Grieger & Boyd, 1980). The distinction is not one of intensity but of quality. Intense levels of appropriate emotions tend to motivate constructive behavior, whereas intense levels of inappropriate emotions tend to be disruptive and counterproductive. The goal is to change the quality of the emotion rather than lower the intensity; otherwise, clients may become indifferent about their problems.

REBT assumes that people are often indoctrinated with basic irrational ideas perpetuated by Western culture (Ellis & Bernard, 1986). Demandingness (an absolutistic "should" or "must") is the core irrational belief that is responsible for human emotional disturbance (Ellis, 1989a). The main irrational ideas they learn and invent are: (1) I must do well and/or be approved by significant others or I am an inadequate person; (2) Others must treat me kindly and fairly or else they are rotten individuals; and (3) Conditions under which I live must be safe and comfortable or else the world is a horrible place in which to live and life is hardly worth living. An irrational absolutistic "must" is the basic premise. Three forms of thinking that are logical derivatives of a basic irrational "must" would be awfulizing, damnation, and I-can't-stand-it-itis. More recently, Ellis (1994) has emphasized a fourth derivative, always-and-never thinking. There can be many variations and corollaries of the basic premise and its logical derivatives.

DiGiuseppe (1991) has noted that it is important to differentiate between inferences or automatic thoughts and core irrational beliefs that an individual may have about the world. A person may have a misperception or irrational idea about an event, which, if corrected, would be helpful to him or her. The more serious problem in RET is a core irrational belief, such as that it should not be this way. A female client incorrectly perceives that some people do not like her. She will feel better to find out that her perception is not accurate. Nevertheless, she may still have a core irrational (demandingness) belief that people should never feel this way about her.

A distinction is also made in RET between ego disturbance and discomfort disturbance (Ellis & Dryden, 1987). In ego disturbance a person makes demands on self, others and the world; and, if these demands are not met, the person becomes disturbed by damning self. In discomfort disturbance the person makes the same demands but they are related to dogmatic commands that comfortable life conditions must exist (low frustration tolerance). Discomfort anxiety is often less dramatic than ego anxiety but is probably more common.

THERAPEUTIC PROCESS

Dryden and DiGiuseppe (1990) describe the ABC framework in REBT as A = the activating event, B = the beliefs, and C = the emotional and behavioral consequences. They outline the following steps in the REBT treatment sequences: (1) Ask for a problem, (2) Define and agree upon a target problem, (3) Assess C, (4) Assess A, (5) Identify and assess any secondary emotional problems, (6) Teach the B–C connection, (7) Assess beliefs, (8) Connect irrational beliefs and C, (9) Dispute irrational beliefs, (10) Prepare to deepen conviction in rational beliefs, (11) Encourage the client to put new learning into practice, (12) Check homework assignments, and (13) Facilitate the working-through process.

Active-directive therapeutic techniques in REBT are generally considered the most effective way to change thoughts, feelings, and behaviors (Ellis & Dryden, 1987; Ellis & Grieger, 1986; Dryden & Trower, 1986). Cognitive, emotive, and behavioral techniques include confrontations, probing, challenging, and disputing irrational beliefs, teaching procedures, giving emotive exercises, and assigning homework tasks. Expressive-emotive-experiential procedures adapted from Gestalt psychology are occasionally used to help clients get in touch with their feelings. Clients are then taught how they create most of their self-destructive emotions by what they are telling themselves.

"Shame-attacking" and "risk-attacking" exercises are considered particularly effective in REBT (Ellis & Dryden, 1987). In shame-attacking exercises, clients deliberately act "shamefully" in public in order to accept themselves and to tolerate the ensuing discomfort. Clients are instructed not to harm themselves or other people, and only minor infractions of social rules are involved (e.g., calling out the time on a crowded subway, wearing bizarre clothes, going into a hardware store and asking if they sell tobacco). Risk-attacking exercises involve clients deliberately forcing themselves to take risks in areas where they wish to make changes (e.g., people who experience shyness forcing themselves to attend social functions).

Ellis (Ellis & Dryden, 1987) believes that an ideal REBT therapist would give unconditional acceptance to a client. However, he encourages a very forceful style and believes that being too warm to a client could possibly be antitherapeutic. Not all REBT therapists concur with this latter view. Ellis admits the REBT can be combined with a "Rogerian" low-key manner and still work (Weinrach, 1980), but he believes it is less effective that way and takes longer. He indicates that there can be different therapeutic styles, as well as techniques borrowed from other therapeutic systems, as long as one does not depart from the principles of REBT.

The therapeutic use of humor is considered helpful in REBT (Ellis, 1994). REBT hypothesizes that almost all neurotic disturbances stem from taking things too seriously. Paradoxical intention, evocative language, irony, wit, cartoons, and rational humorous songs are all used as antidotes to irrational thinking. However, it humorously attacks the client's "beliefs" and not the "client."

Therapy is directed toward three forms of insight: (1) disturbance is primarily determined by absolutistic beliefs, (2) people remain disturbed by reindoctrinating themselves in the present, and (3) change comes about from diligent work and practice. The ultimate goal is not only removal of the clients' symptoms but a change in their basic philosophy of life which will significantly lessen their tendency to disturb themselves. The most elegant and long-lasting changes are ones that involve philosophical restructuring of irrational beliefs.

Clients frequently have secondary emotional problems (and sometimes tertiary problems) about their primary emotional problems (Ellis & Dryden, 1987). A person may feel anxious about failing a test and then feel anxious about feeling anxious and eventually experience panic and hopelessness as a result of the secondary emotional disturbance. It may be necessary to work on the secondary or tertiary problem first if it is significantly interfering with work on the primary problem.

Ellis (1989b) has noted that individuals who are out of contact with reality, in a highly manic state, seriously autistic or brain injured, and in the lower levels of mental deficiency are not normally treated in REBT. Nevertheless, because of its simplicity and clarity, he believes that REBT is more effective with less intelligent, poorly educated, economically deprived, and lower motivated clients than most of the usual psychotherapeutic approaches. Clients with borderline intellectual functioning, for example, may not be suitable candidates for rational restructuring but they have been taught simple coping statements. The reader should refer to Chapter 2 under the section "Mental and Physical Disabilities" for more detailed examples of the types of clients normally treated in REBT.

Although REBT can be presented at a very basic level as brief therapy, it is an approach that can become very complex as therapists work with clients with higher intelligence and education (Ellis, 1989b). REBT becomes significantly more effective and complex with mildly disturbed individuals and those who have a single major symptom. It is a system with only a few parts, but one in which the interaction of those parts can become very complex.

REBT primarily follows an educational model of therapy (Ellis & Harper, 1975). A large variety of educational procedures are employed such as bibliotherapy, homework report sheets, tape recordings, cards with rational statements, diagrams, games and so forth. Ellis and Harper (1975) suggested that the future of psychotherapy may well lie in the development of even better methods of emotional education and indicated that the terms "emotional education" or "tolerance training" may replace the term "psychotherapy." Woods (1991), a university professor, has developed some original materials and approaches that reflect this theme.

RESEARCH AND FURTHER CONSIDERATIONS

Corey (1991) has noted that there are methodological shortcomings in REBT research but that recent reviews have provided evidence for the clinical effectiveness of REBT. Major reviews over a period of years indicate that REBT has generated considerable research (Ellis, 1977; DiGiuseppe & Miller, 1977; McGovern & Silverman, 1984; Silverman, McCarthy, & McGovern, 1992). Silverman, McCarthy and McGovern (1992) stated that their recent review coincided with the previous findings that REBT is a valuable effective therapy that warrants increased research to broaden its application.

Ellis (1989a) has pointed out that most research studies have focused on cognitive restructuring. The cognitive disputing of irrational beliefs is what originally made RET radically different from other psychotherapeutic orientations when it evolved. Nevertheless, REBT has always used cognitive, emotive, and behavioral techniques and is even more comprehensive in that combination in its contemporary form (Ellis, 1991).

When clients are helped to make long-lasting philosophical changes in their irrational beliefs, Ellis considers that to be elegant or preferential REBT (Ellis & Dryden, 1987). However, if it becomes apparent that clients are not able to change their irrational beliefs, the REBT therapist would endeavor to help them change the activating event directly or to change their distorted inferences about the situation. When therapeutic effort is directed in the latter manner, Ellis (Ellis & Dryden, 1987) considers REBT to be synonymous with broad-based cognitive-behavior therapy.

Ellis (1994) originally called his approach Rational Therapy or RT to emphasize the cognitive element. He later changed it to Rational-Emotive Therapy or RET to reflect the emotive element. More recently, he has renamed it Rational Emotive Behavior Therapy because he thought it more accurately described his approach in terms of all three elements.

Recent books that elaborate on the principles of REBT and provide more detail on the practice of REBT include: Bernard (1991), Bernard and Wolfe (1993), Dryden (1990), Dryden and DiGiuseppe (1990), Dryden and Hill (1993), Ellis (1994), Ellis and Abrahms, 1994), Ellis and Velton (1992), Grieger and Woods (1994), Yankura and Dryden (1990), and Walen, DiGiuseppe, and Dryden (1992).

Ellis (Weinrach, 1980) has noted that the film *Three Approaches to Psychotherapy* (Shostrum, 1965) with the client, Gloria, which is the impression that many people have of REBT, never accurately reflected his approach even then. A number of films and videotapes have been developed since then that are a more accurate reflection. A recent production, the *Master's Therapists: Videotaped Sessions* (DiGiuseppe, 1993), depicts therapy sessions by four leading REBT therapists and trainers (Ray DiGiuseppe, Albert Ellis, Janet Wolfe, and Dominic DiMattia).

Further information on the books and videotapes mentioned above as well as additional information on REBT can be obtained from the Institute for Rational-Emotive Therapy, 45 East 65th Street, New York, New York 10021; Phone: (800) 323-IRET or (212) 535-0822.

REFERENCES

Ard, B. N., Jr. (1990). *Guilt and/or blame: Conscience, superego and psychotherapy* (2nd ed.). New York: Peter Lang.

Bernard, M. E. (Ed.). (1991). *Using rational-emotive therapy effectively: A practitioner's guide.* New York: Plenum.

Bernard, M. E., & Wolfe, J. L. (Eds.). (1993). *The RET resource book for practitioners.* New York: Wiley.

Corey, G. (1991). *Theory and practice of counseling and psychotherapy.* (4th ed.). Monterey, CA: Brooks-Cole.

DiGiuseppe, R. (1991). Comprehensive cognitive disputing in RET. In M. E. Bernard (Ed.), *Using rational-emotive therapy effectively: A practitioner's guide.* New York: Plenum.

DiGiuseppe, R. (1993). (Series Ed.). *Master therapists: Videotaped sessions* (Videos). New York: Institute for Rational-Emotive Therapy.

DiGiuseppe, R. A., & Miller, N. J. (1977). A review of outcome studies on rational-emotive therapy. In A. Ellis & R. Grieger (Eds.), *Handbook of rational-emotive therapy.* New York: Springer.

Dryden, W. (1990). *Creativity in rational-emotive therapy.* Loughton, England: Gale Centre.

Dryden, W., & DiGiuseppe, R. (1990). *A primer on rational-emotive therapy.* Champaign, IL: Research.

Dryden, W., & Hill, L. K. (Ed.). (1993). *Innovations in rational-emotive therapy.* Newbury Park, CA: Sage.

Dryden, W., & Trower, P. (Eds.). (1986). *Rational-emotive therapy: Recent developments in theory and practice.* Bristol, England: Institute for RET (UK).

Ellis, A. (1962). *Reason and emotion in psychotherapy.* Secaucus, NJ: Citadel.

Ellis, A. (1973). *Humanistic psychotherapy: The rational-emotive approach.* New York: McGraw-Hill.

Ellis, A. (1977). Research data supporting the clinical and personality hypotheses of RET and other cognitive-behavior therapies. In A. Ellis and R. Grieger (Eds.), *Handbook of rational-emotive psychotherapy.* New York: Springer.

Ellis, A. (1989a). Comments on my critics. In M. E. Bernard & R. DiGiuseppe (Eds.), *Inside rational-emotive therapy: A critical appraisal of the theory and therapy of Albert Ellis.* San Diego: Academic.

Ellis, A. (1989b). Rational-emotive therapy. In R. J. Corsini & D. Wedding (Eds.), *Current psychotherapies* (4th ed.). Itasca, IL: F. E. Peacock.

Ellis, A. (1991). The revised ABC's of rational-emotive therapy (RET). *Journal of Rational-Emotive and Cognitive Behavior Therapy, 9*(3), 139–172.

Ellis, A. (1994). *Reason and emotion in psychotherapy* (2nd ed.). New York: Birch Lane Press (Carol).

Ellis, A., & Abrahams, M. (1994). *How to cope with a fatal illness.* New York: Barricade Books.

Ellis, A., & Bernard, M. E. (1986). What is rational-emotive therapy (RET)? In A. Ellis & R. Grieger (with contributors), *Handbook of rational-emotive therapy, volume II.* New York: Springer.

Ellis, A., & Dryden, W. (1987). *The practice of rational-emotive therapy.* New York: Springer.

Ellis, A., & Grieger, R. M. (Eds.). (1986). *Handbook of rational-emotive therapy, volume 2.* New York: Springer.

Ellis, A., & Harper, R. A. (1975). *A new guide to rational living.* Englewood Cliffs, NJ: Prentice-Hall.

Ellis, A., & Velton, E. (1992). *When AA doesn't work for you: Rational steps to quitting alcohol.* New York: Barricade Books.

Grieger, R. M., & Boyd, J. (1980). *Rational-emotive therapy: A skills-based approach.* New York: Van Nostrand Reinhold.

Grieger, R. M., & Woods, P. J. (1993). *The rational-emotive therapy companion.* Roanoke, VA: Scholars Press.

Hauck, P. A. (1992). *Overcoming the rating game: Beyond self-love — beyond self-esteem.* Louisville, KY: Westminster/John Knox.

McGovern, T., & Silverman, M. (1984). A review of outcome studies on rational-emotive therapy. *Journal of Rational-Emotive Therapy, 2,* 7–18.

Shostrum, E. (Producer). (1965). *Three approaches to psychotherapy* (Part 3) (Film). Wheeler, CA: Psychological Films, Inc.

Silverman, M. S., McCarthy, M., & McGovern, T. (1992). A review of outcome studies of rational-emotive therapy from 1982–1989. *Journal of Rational-Emotive Therapy, 10*(3), 11–175.

Walen, S. R., DiGiuseppe, R., & Dryden, W. (1992). *A practitioner's guide to rational-emotive therapy.* New York: Oxford University Press.

Weinrach, S. G. (1980). Unconventional therapist: Albert Ellis. *Personnel and Guidance Journal, 59*(3), 152–160.

Wessler, R. A., & Wessler, R. L. (1980). *The principles and practice of rational-emotive therapy.* San Francisco, CA: Jossey-Bass.

Woods, P. J. (1991). Orthodox RET taught effectively with graphics, feedback on irrational beliefs, a structured homework series, and models of disputation. In M. E. Bernard (Ed.), *Using rational-emotive therapy effectively: A practitioner's guide.* New York: Plenum.

Yankura, J., & Dryden, W. (1990). *Doing RET: Albert Ellis in action.* New York: Springer.

Chapter 2

MENTAL HEALTH REHABILITATION
AND RATIONAL EMOTIVE BEHAVIOR THERAPY
(REBT)

M ental health rehabilitation is defined as therapeutic counseling designed to facilitate the emotional development of individuals with mental and physical disabilities that enables them to lead more productive lives. Productivity is considered to include avocational as well as vocational activities. This definition describes the type of therapeutic counseling that is performed by rehabilitation counselors (Gandy, Martin, Hardy, & Cull, 1987; Gandy, Martin, & Hardy, in press; Hardy, 1991; Martin & Gandy, 1990). As indicated in the preface, it is also applicable to a wide variety of other disciplines involved with the therapeutic counseling of people with disabilities.

Rehabilitation counselor training also focuses on the total rehabilitation process and the holistic nature of people with disabilities (Jarrell, Hardy & Martin, 1987; Martin & Gandy, 1990; McDowell, in press; Lassiter, Lassiter, Hardy, Underwood, & Cull, 1983; Lawton, 1981; Wright, 1987). Educational, vocational, and avocational aspects are emphasized as well as personal and social concerns. Although some rehabilitation counselors specialize in therapeutic counseling and even become licensed to provide it in private practice, many will focus on the therapeutic aspect of rehabilitation counseling in varying degrees (Gandy et al., in press; Hardy, Luck, & Chandler, 1982). The discussion in this chapter will emphasize the therapeutic counseling aspect, although the holistic aspects will be represented, as also will be reflected in the case studies in Part Two.

BACKGROUND AND CONSIDERATIONS

Ard (1968) initially introduced the idea of REBT in rehabilitation counseling in the therapeutic counseling of people with disabilities. The

14

initial reaction was negative because of some major misperceptions of REBT (Gandy, 1985, 1994b). REBT was viewed as neglecting emotions, imposing values, neglecting the therapeutic relationship, and being effective only with highly intelligent and educated individuals. As indicated in the overview of REBT in Chapter 1, this view was not accurate.

Weinrach (1982) noted REBT initially experienced a lack of acceptance in therapeutic counseling in general largely because of Albert Ellis's personal style, which entertains some and alienates others. He further noted that there are many myths about Ellis and his life-style. Two interview articles (Dryden, 1989; Weinrach, 1980) and a book of anecdotes by colleagues, students, and friends (DiMattia & Lega, 1990) help to provide a more accurate perspective about Albert Ellis. As DiMattia commented, "Is he the brusque individual of his public persona? Yes, he is that. But he is much more. . . . Albert Ellis is, above all, a human being: sensitive, caring, funny, supportive, eccentric, energetic, dedicated; more interested in helping others than in being 'liked' " (DiMattia & Lega, p. 9).

As noted in Chapter 1, although REBT can become very complex, it is an approach that can be presented at a basic level as brief therapy. Ellis and Abrams (1978) have demonstrated that REBT encourages relatively short-term therapy by stressing directness, a high degree of activity by the therapist, bibliotherapy, and specific homework assignments for clients to perform in between the REBT sessions. They believe that the basic principles and practice can be quickly learned and easily applied in the form of brief therapy by health care professionals.

An effective short-term approach to therapy is very helpful to rehabilitation counselors and related professionals performing therapeutic counseling functions in agency settings where they experience considerable time constraints (Gandy et al., 1987; Gandy et al., in press; Martin & Gandy, 1990). Rehabilitation counselors and related professionals in the private practice of therapeutic counseling can also benefit from a brief therapy model because of the increasing emphasis on such procedures by third-party insurance carriers.

As indicated in Chapter 1, REBT is primarily an educational model. The educational emphasis is very compatible with rehabilitation counselor training, as well as related disciplines involved with the therapeutic counseling of people with disabilities that operate from more of a behavioral or educational model (Gandy, 1985; Gandy & Rule, 1983; Lassiter, 1983). The structured and organized problem-solving nature of

REBT provides a clarity and specificity that is similar to methods and procedures that have been associated with the successful rehabilitation of people with disabilities.

MENTAL AND PHYSICAL DISABILITIES

The fourth edition of the American Psychiatric Association's *Diagnostic and Statistical Manual of Mental Disorders* (*DSM-IV*) (1994) notes that to make a distinction between "mental disorders" and "physical disorders" is a reductionistic anachronism of mind/body dualism. "A compelling literature documents that there is much 'physical' in 'mental' disorders and much 'mental' in 'physical' disorders" (American Psychiatric Association, 1994, p. xxi). The *DSM-IV* further notes that the term "mental" disorders has been much clearer than its solution, and the term persists because an appropriate substitute has not been found.

The above message of the *DSM-IV* is important to keep in mind in the following discussion of the application of REBT to what are traditionally considered "mental" and "physical" disabilities.

REBT and Mental Disabilities

Chapter 1 noted that individuals who are out of contact with reality, in a highly manic state, seriously autistic or brain injured, and in the lower ranges of mental deficiency are not normally treated in REBT. However, Ellis (1989) also notes that most other individuals with difficulties are treated with REBT and include: clients with maladjustment, moderate anxiety, or marital problems; those with sexual difficulties; run-of-the-mill "neurotics"; individuals with character disorders; truants; juvenile delinquents and adult criminals; borderline personalities; overt psychotics, including those with delusions and hallucinations, when they are somewhat in contact with reality; individuals with higher grade mental deficiency; and clients with psychosomatic problems.

A considerable literature exists on the application of REBT to mental disorders; consequently, only selected references will be mentioned. Case studies and detailed discussions on neurotic reactions, psychotic conditions in partial remission, severe personality disorders, substance-related disorders, sexual difficulties, relationship concerns, marriage and family issues, childhood problems, and so forth were provided early in the development of REBT (e.g., Ellis, 1957, 1958, 1960, 1962, 1965,

1971). More recent literature on such clinical disturbances as well as newer formulations exists (e.g., Bernard & Joyce, 1991, 1994; Ellis, 1988, 1994a, 1994b, 1994c, 1994d; Ellis, McInerney, DiGiuseppe & Yeager, 1988; Ellis, Sichel, Yeager, DiMattia & DiGiuseppe, 1989; Ellis & Velton, 1992; Huber & Baruth, 1989; Trimpey, 1989; Warren & Zgourides, 1991; Wolfe, 1992).

Ellis et al. (1988) report that alcohol abuse is the world's number one health problem. An innovative development in REBT has been the development of Rational Recovery (RR) (Ellis & Velton, 1992; Trimpey, 1989). RR is a self-help program for people wanting abstinence from alcohol or other drugs that is offered as an alternative, not a competitor, to the traditional model of Alcoholics Anonymous (AA). Although many members of RR have spiritual beliefs, the main distinction between RR and AA is that RR is not spiritually focused. For those who prefer AA, DiMattia (1991) has noted that many REBT concepts in themselves are very complementary to a spiritual focus. Ellis (1985) has pointed out that there are several steps in the AA 12-step program that help individuals significantly.

Although most of the REBT literature is devoted to adults with mental disorders, Bernard and Joyce (1991, 1994) have noted that REBT now has a long history of application with children and adolescents. REBT has been applied to a variety of childhood problems including conduct disorders, low frustration tolerance, impulsivity, academic underachievement, anxieties, fears and phobias, social isolation, obesity, and childhood sexuality. An active-directive, confrontational style of REBT has frequently been encouraged with adults, but an emphasis on relationship building has been the focus of REBT with children and adolescents.

Ellis (1994c) recently published a revision of his 1962 edition of *Reason and Emotion in Psychotherapy*, but omitted detailed chapters on specific therapy problems because of space limitations. He is currently working on Volume 2, which will include revised formulations of case studies in the first edition such as dating, marriage and family issues, sex problems, and the treatment of severe personality disorders. He indicated that Volume 2 will probably be entitled *Rational Emotive Behavior Therapy with Clinical Problems: Volume 2 of Reason and Emotion in Psychotherapy.*

REBT and Physical Disabilities

Sweetland (1990) has noted that people with physical disabilities are not necessarily more disturbed or irrational in their thinking than other people, but irrational attitudes can exacerbate physical disabilities. He believes there are at least three reasons why a cognitive approach is particularly appropriate when assisting people with physical disabilities: (1) the disability is permanent and only one's reaction to it, not the condition itself, can be modified; (2) many people hold extremely irrational attitudes toward physical disabilities; and (3) since people with a physical disability can rarely, if ever, attain a sense of physical mastery, a sense of cognitive mastery and control may be even more important for this population than the general population.

Sweetland (1990) further observed that a common irrational belief among people with severe physical disabilities is that the disability is really awful, terrible and catastrophic. Another common belief is the alternate belief, sometimes referred to as reaction formation or denial, which is a defense against the underlying belief that having a disability is catastrophic. People with severe physical disabilities also frequently have the unrealistic belief, "I have paid my dues." The corollary of the latter belief is that since something catastrophic has already happened in my life, nothing very bad should happen again. A similar belief is the idea that somehow the world should make up for the problems that the disability causes. A variation is the idea, "Since I have a physical disability, I can't be expected to do much."

Calabro (1990) has developed a three-phase cognitive-behavioral model for analyzing and facilitating the adjustment process which follows severe physical disability. The "pre-encounter phase" is the first stage and immediately follows the onset of incapacitating disability. Shock and denial are characteristic of the first stage, and the individual has not acknowledged that an activating or disabling event has occurred. The second stage or "post-encounter phase" involves acknowledgment of the disabling condition by the patient, and periods of anxiety, depression, and expressed anger are common. Early treatment is better focussed on managing the patient's environment and on direct cognitive intervention with beliefs held by the rehabilitation team. The "rational re-encounter phase," or final stage, is characterized by repeated re-encounters with various forms of the disabling activating event and anticipated activating events. During the final stage, the patient is more able to benefit from direct cognitive intervention tailored to the specific pattern of irrational beliefs often associated with disability.

Wallace and Maddox (1978) have also discussed the usefulness of REBT with people with physical disabilities. Lichtenberg, Johnson, and Arachtingi (1992) found a significant relationship between persons' subscription to irrational beliefs and their susceptibility to physical illness. REBT literature on some specific physical disabilities includes cancer (Golden & Gersh, 1990), coronary heart disease (Lohr & Hamberger, 1990), diabetes (Rubin, Walen, & Ellis, 1990), low back pain, peptic ulcer, and migraine headache (Forman, Tosi, & Rudy, 1987), psychosomatic disorders (Woods, 1987a, 1987b; Woods & Burns, 1984; Woods & Lyons, 1990), renal disease (Fisher, 1976) and visual disabilities (Needham & Ehmer, 1980). Oliver and Block (1987, 1990) have developed guidelines for the caregiver in coping with Alzheimer's disease patients, which is also helpful for dealing with any person who is chronically ill or has a severe disability. Some of the references mentioned thus far under REBT and physical disabilities can be found in two special issues of the *Journal of Rational-Emotive and Cognitive Behavior Therapy* (Grieger, 1990a, 1990b).

Ellis (1981) applied REBT to thanatology many years ago. Recently, he has expanded on these ideas, in collaboration with Michael Abrams, and published a book entitled *How to Cope with a Fatal Illness: The Rational Management of Death and Dying* (Ellis & Abrams, 1994). They explain how people with terminal cancer, AIDS, or other death-dealing afflictions can learn to cope and enjoy their remaining days. They note how friends and loved ones may have a harmful influence if they panic over impending death. Examples of well-known individuals and ones who are not well known are provided.

MENTAL HEALTH REHABILITATION APPLICATIONS

Some mental health rehabilitation concepts and strategies in the rehabilitation counseling discipline that incorporate REBT principles and techniques have been developed over time. These concepts and strategies have been applied to mental and/or physical disabilities.

As previously mentioned, Ard (1968) initially introduced the concept of REBT in rehabilitation counseling in the therapeutic counseling of people with disabilities. He pointed out how it could be a helpful approach with rehabilitation clients whose disabilities have helped to exacerbate their frustrations with themselves, other people, and the world. Otsby (1985) later observed that REBT could be useful in rehabilitation counseling with a wide variety of clientele. He pointed out that REBT is appropriate for individuals who retain some ability to accurately perceive reality and who are able to understand the concept or the relationship between thoughts, feelings, and behavior (e.g., if I think this way, I end up feeling and acting in certain ways). Gandy (1985, 1994a, 1994b) has noted frequent misperceptions of REBT and how REBT can better be incorporated into the rehabilitation counselor education curriculum.

Lassiter (1983) developed a model that combined Adlerian life-style counseling with REBT as it related to work adjustment techniques with people with severe physical disabilities. He noted that an important feature of REBT is that it incorporates a concept of closure, or graduation from therapy, to a continuing self-instructional program of learning. From a rehabilitation perspective, this is a beginning for clients to work toward independence now that they are equipped to deal effectively with unconstructive emotions they are bound to experience during work.

Gandy and Rule (1983) demonstrated how REBT can be applied to group counseling with clients with severe physical disabilities. Gandy (1992, 1995) described how a systematic written homework self-help technique of disputing irrational beliefs can be utilized as a brief therapy stress management technique in the emotional adjustment of clients with physical or mental disabilities. Gandy's (1979) discussion regarding frustration with individuals who exploit other people is relevant to people with disabilities who are vulnerable to such behavior. Gandy (1987) has also discussed the application of REBT to clients with chemical dependency and their families. Rule (1977) reported on how a self-modeled humor exercise involving a combination of the Adlerian and REBT approaches could increase self-awareness and self-acceptance. Rule (1980) also developed a rational apothecary, or brief guideline, for when to use various rational techniques. Rule (1983) and Sweeney (1989) have developed practioner oriented books on Adlerian counseling techniques, which are useful resources for techniques that are highly compatible with REBT techniques in the mental health rehabilitation of clients with mental and/or physical disabilities.

REFERENCES

American Psychiatric Association. (1994). *Diagnostic and statistical manual of mental disorders (DSM-IV)* (4th ed.). Washington, D.C.: American Psychiatric Association.

Ard, B. N., Jr. (1968). Rational therapy in rehabilitation counseling. *Rehabilitation Counseling Bulletin, 12*(2), 84–88.

Bernard, M. E., & Joyce, M. R. (1991). RET with children and adolescents. In M. E. Bernard (Ed.), *Using rational-emotive therapy effectively: A practitioner's guide.* New York: Plenum.

Bernard, M. E., & Joyce, M. R. (1994). *Rational-emotive therapy with children and adolescents* (2nd ed.). New York: Wiley.

Calabro, Louis E. (1990). Adjustment to disability: A cognitive-behavioral model for analysis and clinical management. *Journal of Rational-Emotive and Cognitive-Behavior Therapy, 8*(2), 79–102.

DiMattia, D. (1991). Using RET effectively in the workplace. In M. E. Bernard (Ed.), *Using rational-emotive therapy effectively: A practitioner's guide.* New York: Plenum.

DiMattia, D., & Lega, L. (Eds.). (1990). *Will the real Albert Ellis stand up?* New York: Institute for Rational-Emotive Therapy.

Dryden, W. (1989). Albert Ellis: An efficient and passionate life. *Journal of Counseling and Development, 67*(10), 539–546.

Ellis, A. (1957). *How to live with a neurotic: At home and at work.* New York: Crown, rev. ed.; Hollywood, CA: Wilshire, 1975.

Ellis, A. (1958). *Sex without guilt.* New York: Lyle Stuart, rev. ed.: New York: Lyle Stuart, 1965.

Ellis, A. (1960). *The art and science of love.* Secaucus, NJ: Lyle Stuart.

Ellis, A. (1962). *Reason and emotion in psychotherapy.* Secaucus, NJ: Citadel.

Ellis, A. (1965). *The treatment of borderline and psychotic individuals.* New York: Institute for Rational-Emotive Therapy, rev. ed., 1988.

Ellis, A. (1971). *Growth through reason.* Palo Alto, CA: Science and Behavior Books.

Ellis, A. (1981). The rational-emotive approach to thanatology. In H. J. Sobel (Ed.), *Behavior therapy in terminal care.* Cambridge, MA: Ballinger.

Ellis, A. (1985). Rational-emotive approach to acceptance and its relationship to EAP's. In S. H. Klarreich, J. L. Francek, & C. E. Moore (Eds.), *The human resource management handbook: Principles and practice of employee assistance programs.* New York: Praeger.

Ellis, A. (1988). *How to stubbornly refuse to make yourself miserable about anything—yes anything!.* Secaucus, NJ: Lyle Stuart.

Ellis A. (1989). Comments on my critics. In M. E. Bernard & R. DiGiuseppe (Eds.), *Inside rational-emotive therapy: A critical appraisal of the theory and therapy of Albert Ellis.* San Diego: Academic.

Ellis, A. (1994a). Rational emotive behavior therapy approaches to obsessive-compulsive disorder (OCD). *Journal of Rational-Emotive and Cognitive-Behavior Therapy, 12*(2), 121–141.

Ellis, A. (1994b). Post-traumatic stress disorder (PYSD): A rational emotive behavioral theory. *Journal of Rational-Emotive and Cognitive-Behavior Therapy, 12*(1), 3–26.

Ellis, A. (1994c). *Reason and emotion in psychotherapy.* New York: Birch Lane Press (Carol).

Ellis, A. (1994d). The treatment of borderline personalities with rational emotive behavior therapy. *Journal of Rational-Emotive and Cognitive-Behavior Therapy, 12*(2), 101–120.

Ellis, A., & Abrams, E. (1978). *Brief psychotherapy in medical and health practice.* New York: Springer.

Ellis, A., & Abrams, M. (1994). *How to cope with a fatal illness.* New York: Barricade Books.

Ellis, A., McInerney, J. F., DiGiuseppe, R., & Yeager, R. J. (1988). *Rational-emotive therapy with alcoholics and substance abusers.* Needham, MA: Allyn & Bacon.

Ellis, A., Sichel, J. L., Yeager, R. J., DiMattia, D. J., & DiGiuseppe, R. A. (1989). *Rational-emotive couples therapy.* Needham, MA: Allyn & Bacon.

Ellis, A., & Velton, E. (1992). *When AA doesn't work for you: Rational steps for quitting alcohol.* New York: Barricade Books.

Fisher, S. (1976). The renal dialysis client: A rational counseling approach. *Rehabilitation Counseling Bulletin, 19*(4), 556–562.

Forman, M. A., Tosi, D. S. J., & Rudy, D. R. (1987). Common irrational beliefs associated with the psychophysiological conditions of low back pain, peptic ulcers, and migraine headache: A multivariate study. *Journal of Rational-Emotive Therapy, 5,* 255–265.

Gandy, G. L. (1979). An alternate approach to loving or hating your enemies. *The Humanist Educator, 17*(4), 153–159.

Gandy, G. L. (1985). Frequent misperceptions of rational-emotive therapy: An overview for the rehabilitation counselor. *Journal of Applied Rehabilitation Counseling, 16*(4), 31–35.

Gandy, G. L. (1987). Rational-emotive therapy: A creative way to enhance emotions. *The Addiction Letter* (Manisses Communications Group, Inc.), *3*(2), 1–2.

Gandy, G. L. (1992, September). *Disputing irrational beliefs in rehabilitation counseling.* Paper presented at the Fourth International Conference on Stress Management, Paris, France.

Gandy, G. L. (1994a, April). REBT and rehabilitation counselor education. In S. G. Weinrach (Chair), *Infusing REBT concepts into the counselor preparation curriculum.* Panel conducted at the annual meeting of the American Counseling Association, Minneapolis, Minnesota.

Gandy, G. L. (1994, July). *Rational emotive behavior therapy in rehabilitation counseling.* Paper presented at the 23rd International Congress of Applied Psychology, Madrid, Spain.

Gandy, G. L. (1995). Disputing irrational beliefs in rehabilitation counseling. *Journal of Applied Rehabilitation Rehabilitation Counseling, 26*(1), 39–40.

Gandy, G. L., Martin, E. D., Jr., and Hardy, R. E. (Authors/Editors). (in press). *Counseling and the rehabilitation process: Mental and physical disabilities.* Springfield, IL: Charles C Thomas.

Gandy, G. L., Martin, E. D., Jr., Hardy, R. E., and Cull, J. G. (Authors/Editors). (1987). *Rehabilitation counseling and services: Profession and process.* Springfield, IL: Charles C Thomas.

Gandy, G. L., and Rule, W. R. (1983). The use of group counseling. In R. A. Lassiter, M. H. Lassiter, R. E. Hardy, J. W. Underwood, & J. G. Cull (Eds.), *Vocational evaluation, work adjustment, and independent living services for disabled people.* Springfield, IL: Charles C Thomas.

Grieger, R. M. (Ed.). (1990a). Cognitive behavior therapy with physically ill people: Part 1. (Special issue). *Journal of Rational-Emotive and Cognitive-Behavior Therapy, 8*(1).

Grieger, R. M. (Ed.). (1990b). Cognitive behavior therapy with physically ill people: Part 2. (Special issue). *Journal of Rational-Emotive and Cognitive-Behavior Therapy, 8*(1).

Golden, W. L., & Gersh, W. D. (1990). Cognitive behavior therapy in the treatment of cancer patients. *Journal of Rational-Emotive and Cognitive-Behavior Therapy, 8*(1), 41–52.

Hardy, R. E. (1991). *Gestalt psychotherapy: Concepts and demonstrations in stress, relationships, hypnosis and addiction.* Springfield, IL: Charles C Thomas.

Hardy, R. E., Luck, R. S., & Chandler, A. L. (1982). Licensure of rehabilitation counselors and related issues: Results of a national survey. *Rehabilitation Counseling Bulletin, 25*(3), 157–161.

Huber, C. H., & Baruth, L. G. (1989). *Rational-emotive and systems family therapy.* New York: Springer.

Jarrell, G. R., Hardy, R. E., & Martin, E. D., Jr. (1987). Occupational analysis and placement. In G. L. Gandy, E. D. Martin, Jr., R. E. Hardy, & J. G. Cull (Authors/Editors), *Rehabilitation counseling and services: Profession and process.* Springfield, IL: Charles C Thomas.

Lassiter, R. A. (1983). Work adjustment techniques in lifestyle counseling. In W. R. Rule (Ed.), *Lifestyle counseling for adjustment to disability.* Rockville, MD: Aspen.

Lassiter, R. A., Lassiter, M. H., Hardy, R. E., Underwood, J. W., & Cull, J. G. (1983). *Vocational evaluation, work adjustment, and independent living for severely disabled people.* Springfield, IL: Charles C Thomas.

Lawton, M. J. (1981). *The role of the rehabilitation counselor as a facilitative gatekeeper for the alcoholic and licit drug abuser* (Rehabilitation Monograph Series, No. V). Richmond, VA: Virginia Commonwealth University, Department of Rehabilitation Counseling.

Lichtenberg, W. L., Johnson, D. D., & Arachtingi, B. M. (1992). Physical Illness and subscription to Ellis's irrational beliefs. *Journal of Counseling & Development, 71*(2), 157–163.

Lohr, J. M., & Hamberger, L. K. (1990). Cognitive-behavioral modification of coronary-prone behaviors: Proposal for a treatment model and review of the evidence. *Journal of Rational-Emotive and Cognitive-Behavioral Therapy, 8*(2), 103–126.

Martin, E. D., Jr., & Gandy, G. L. (1990). *Rehabilitation and disability: Psychosocial case studies.* Springfield, IL: Charles C Thomas.

McDowell, W. J., Jr. (in press). Intervention strategies with addictions: Is the classic model manageable in a managed care environment? *The Addiction Letter* (Manisses Communications Group, Inc.).

Needham, W. E., & Ehmer, M. N. (1980). RET and adjustment to blindness. *Rational living, 15*(2), 27–32.

Oliver, R., & Bock, F. P. (1987). *Coping with Alzheimer's: A caregiver's emotional survival guide.* North Hollywood, CA: Wilshire.

Oliver, R., & Bock, F. P. (1990). Alleviating the distress of caregivers of Alzheimer's disease patients: A rational-emotive therapy model. *Journal of Rational-Emotive and Cognitive-Behavior Therapy, 8*(1), 53–69.

Otsby, S. S. (1985). A rational-emotive perspective. *Journal of Applied Rehabilitation Counseling, 16*(3), 30–33.

Rubin, R., Walen, S. R., & Ellis, A. (1990). Living with diabetes. *Journal of Rational-Emotive and Cognitive-Behavior Therapy, 8*(1), 21–40.

Rule, W. R. (1977). Increasing self-modeled humor. *Rational Living, 12*(1), 7–9.

Rule, W. R. (1980). What next after self-awareness?: A rational apothecary. *Rational Living, 15*(2), 24–25.

Rule, W. R. (Ed.). (1983). *Lifestyle counseling for adjustment to disability.* Rockville, MD: Aspen.

Sweeney, T. J. (1989). *Adlerian counseling: A practical approach for a new decade* (3rd Edition). Muncie, IN: Accelerated Development.

Sweetland, J. D. (1990). Cognitive-behavior therapy and physical disability. *Journal of Rational-Emotive and Cognitive-Behavior Therapy, 8*(2), 71–78.

Trimpey, J. (1989). *Rational recovery from alcoholism: The small book.* New York: Delacorte.

Wallace, W. A., & Maddox, E. N. (1978). Rational-emotive theory. In W. A. McDowell & A. B. Coven (Eds.), *Counseling theories applied to rehabilitation.* New York: Human Sciences Press.

Warren, R., & Zgourides, G. D. (1991). *Anxiety disorders: A rational-emotive perspective.* Des Moines, IA: Longwood (Allyn & Bacon).

Weinrach, S. G. (1980). Unconventional therapist: Albert Ellis. *Personnel and Guidance Journal, 59*(3), 152–160.

Weinrach, S. G. (1982). Confessions of a novice rational-emotive therapist. *Rational Living, 17*(1), 17–22.

Wolfe, J. L. (1992). *What to do when he has a headache.* New York: Hyperion.

Woods, P. J. (1987a). Do you really want to maintain that a flat tire can upset your stomach? Using the findings of psychophysiology of stress to bloster the argument that people are not directly disturbed by events. *Journal of Rational-Emotive Therapy, 5,* 149–161.

Woods, P. J. (1987b). Reductions in type A behavior, anxiety, anger, and physical illness as related to changes in irrational beliefs: Results of a demonstration project in industry. *Journal of Rational-Emotive Therapy, 5,* 213–237.

Woods, P. J., & Burns, J. (1984). Type A behavior and illness in general. *Journal of Behavioral Medicine, 7,* 411–415.

Woods, P. J., & Lyons, L. C. (1990). Irrational beliefs and psychosomatic disorders. *Journal of Rational-Emotive and Cognitive-Behavior Therapy, 8*(1), 3–20.

Wright, K. C. (1987). The rehabilitation process and professional identity. In G. L. Gandy, E. D. Martin, Jr., R. E. Hardy, & J. G. Cull (Authors/Editors), *Rehabilitation counseling and services: Profession and process.* Springfield, IL: Charles C Thomas.

Chapter 3

DISPUTING IRRATIONAL BELIEFS: THE USE OF SYSTEMATIC WRITTEN HOMEWORK (SWH)

A very helpful procedure in REBT is the use of systematic written homework (SWH) (Ellis, 1971, pp. 182–185; Maultsby, 1971, 1974). As a supplement to individual and/or group therapy sessions, it often helps people to make more rapid progress. It is a writing assignment in which a person is given instructions regarding the application of REBT principles to his or her emotional problem. Many variations of this procedure exists. Forms can be purchased from the Institute for Rational-Emotive Therapy (45 East 65th Street, New York, New York 10021; Phone: (800) 323-IRET or (212) 535-0822) that apply REBT principles in various formats (Ellis & Dryden, 1987; Ellis, 1988; Sichel & Ellis, 1984).

Although a form is helpful, a procedure based on the various formats referred to above that would focus on the disputing of irrational beliefs would be to ask the client to do a writing assignment on notebook paper in which he or she follows an A–B–C–D–E model (Walen, DiGiuseppe, & Dryden, 1992, p. 260). Based on various representations, the following definitions are offered:

A = Activating event or experience that a client has become disturbed about.
B = Beliefs about the event including:
(rB) initial rational beliefs
(iB) subsequent irrational beliefs
C = Consequences of the client's irrational beliefs about the activating experience that are the inappropriate emotional reactions as well as self-defeating behavioral reactions.
D = Disputing, questioning, or challenging of the irrational ideas.
E = the effects of disputing irrational beliefs including:
(cE) the cognitive effects or disputation responses.
(eE) the emotive effect or more appropriate emotions

(bE) the behavioral effect or more constructive behaviors (usually synonymous with future homework assignments)

As indicated in Chapter 1, demandingness (an absolutistic should or must) is the core irrational belief that is responsible for human emotional disturbance (Ellis, 1989). It is important to differentiate between the core irrational belief and an inference or automatic thought. The main core irrational ideas involve demands about self, others and the world/life conditions. Three possible derivatives of a core irrational demand include awfulizing, damnation, and I-can't-stand-it-itis. There can be many variations and corollaries of the basic premise and its logical derivatives, especially depending on the content of the specific activating event.

A helpful scheme for identifying possible irrational belief combinations based on the above rationale is as follows:

   I. Core irrational belief: demands about self (Example: I must do well and be approved by significant others). Logical derivatives:
It is awful if I don't do well and be approved.
I'm inadequate if I don't do well and be approved.
I can't stand it if I don't do well and be approved.

  II. Core irrational belief: demands about others (Example: Others must treat me fairly).
Logical derivatives:
It is awful if I am not treated fairly by others.
Others should be condemned for not treating me fairly.
I can't stand it if I'm not treated fairly.

III. Core irrational belief: demands about the world/life conditions (Example: Life conditions must be the way I want them to be).
Logical derivatives:
It is awful if life is not the way I want it.
Life is rotten if it is not the way I want it.
I can't stand it if life is not the way I want it.

COMPREHENSIVE COGNITIVE DISPUTING

DiGiuseppe (1991) has developed a comprehensive cognitive disputing model that would very much enhance one's use of SWH. He has noted that clients usually have one of the core irrational beliefs and may have one or more derivatives. He suggests that it is best to dispute all four levels of the irrational thoughts processes (core and derivatives) that a client endorses about a particular activating event because one cannot assume generalizations across belief processes. Also, challenging each irrational belief with four disputing strategies—logical, empirical, pragmatic, and construction of a rational belief—is more likely to help a person give up his or her irrational beliefs.

Other features of DiGiuseppe's (1991) cognitive disputing model include the level of abstraction and rhetorical style. Irrational beliefs have varying levels of abstraction. After disputing at a concrete level, moving to an abstract level helps to generalize the learning. Communications may need to move up and down the ladder of abstraction in order to be clearly understood. Disputing styles such as didactic, socratic, metaphorical, and humorous are also helpful in cognitive disputing. The level of abstraction and rhetorical style would tend to be more important in direct therapeutic contact with the client and in the preparation and follow up of the SWH.

Incorporating features of DiGiuseppe's cognitive disputing model (primarily the levels of irrational processes and the disputing strategies) into the systematic written homework technique, an example is presented below in which a client has one of the core irrational beliefs (demands about world/life conditions) and all three of the possible derivatives:

SYSTEMATIC WRITTEN HOMEWORK EXAMPLE

A. Client is a counselor employed in a community agency and is experiencing a very frustrating job experience:

1. Too much emphasis on paperwork and numbers rather than quality counseling with clients.
2. Input from counselors not valued highly by management.
3. Professional development (skill development, research, etc.) not encouraged.
4. Resources for supplies and materials are not adequate.

rB. 1. It would be better if the job was not this way.
2. This is not a pleasant job situation.
3. There are bad features to this job.
4. I don't like this job situation.

iB. 1. The job shouldn't be this way.
2. It is awful that the job is this way.

  3. This is a rotten job.

  4. I can't stand this job.

C. Emotional:

  1. Intense anger (related to iB # 1, 2 & 3).

  2. Intense depression (related to iB # 3 & 4).

Behavioral:

  1. Complaining behavior that is not constructive.

  2. Quality of work has become inconsistent.

D. Disputing of irrational belief # 1: The job shouldn't be this way.

D # 1 (logical dispute) Where is the logic that the job shouldn't be this way?

cE # 1: There is no reason why the job shouldn't be this way because it is this way.

D # 2 (empirical dispute) Where is the evidence that the job shouldn't be this way?

cE # 2: The reality is that there are many examples of similar situations in the world. There is no rule or law of the universe against it.

D # 3 (pragmatic dispute) How will holding the belief that the job shouldn't be this way help you with your future goals?

cE # 3: It will create anger that will exhaust me and prevent me from thinking clearly about the situation and how to improve it.

D # 4 (construction rational belief) What is an alternate belief that would better help me with my future goals?

cE # 4: It would be better if the job was not this way. However, this is reality for me. I would be better off to try to think of realistic ways to improve the situation.

eE of cE's of D's of iB # 1: Intense frustration about the reality of this job situation.

Disputing of irrational belief # 2: It is awful that the job is this way.

D # 1 (logical dispute) Where is the logic that it is awful that the job is this way?

cE # 1: It is bad that the job is this way but that does not make it awful.

D # 2 (empirical dispute) Where is the evidence that it is awful that the job is this way?

cE # 2: The evidence is that the negative features of the job make it very uncomfortable but that is not the same as awful.

D # 3 (pragmatic dispute) How will holding the belief that it is awful that the job is this way help you with your future goals?

cE # 3: It will cause me to focus on the negative features of the job rather than the positive features.

D # 4 (construction rational belief) What is an alternative belief that will better help me with my future goals?

cE # 4: It is bad that the negative features of this job make it very uncomfortable. However, it would be better for me to focus on the positive features of the job.

eE of cE's of D's of iB # 2: Intense anger at the negative features of the job but not at the job.

Disputing of irrational belief # 3: This is a rotten job.

D # 1 (logical) Where is the logic that this is a rotten job?

cE # 1: It is a job with negative features but it doesn't make sense to define the job as rotten.

D # 2 (empirical) Where is the evidence that the job is rotten?

cE # 2: The evidence is that the job has negative features but it also has positive features (for example, it pays my bills).

D # 3 (pragmatic dispute) How will holding the belief that this is a rotten job help me achieve my future goals?

cE # 3: It will consume me with emotions that will prevent me from looking for the positive features of the job and how to capitalize upon them.

D # 4 (construction rational belief) What is an alternative rational belief that will better help me with my future goals?

cE # 4: It is not logical to define the job as rotten. It is a job with negative and positive features. I would be better off to look for the positive features and try to capitalize upon them.

eE of cE's of D's of iB # 3: Intense anger and sadness about the negative features of the job but not about the job.

Disputing of irrational belief # 4: I can't stand it that the job is this way.

D # 1 (logical dispute) Where is the logic that I can't stand it that the job is this way?

cE # 1: I very much don't like the negative features of this job, but that doesn't mean that I can't stand it.

D # 2 (empirical dispute) Where is the evidence that I can't stand that the job is this way?

cE # 2: It is very uncomfortable but the only way it can affect my mental or physical health is by my upsetting myself about it.

D # 3 (pragmatic dispute) How will holding the belief that I can't stand that the job is this way help me achieve my future goals?

cE # 3: It won't help me achieve my future goals because it will depress me and cause me to be immobilized.

D # 4 (construction rational belief) What is an alternative belief that would better help me achieve my future goals?

cE # 4: I very much don't like the negative features of this job and it is very uncomfortable. However, I can stand it and begin to explore ways that I might be able to make the job more comfortable.

eE of cE's of D's of iB # 4: Intense sadness about the discomfort of this job situation.

bE. Homework Assignments:

1. Practice Rational-Emotive Imagery with the irrational beliefs indicated above.

2. Accomplish a future SWH assignment with the goal of generalizing the learning at a more abstract level.

3. Focus on the more positive aspect of the job (such as good relationships with certain co-workers, enjoyable features of the job, practical fringe benefits, etc.).

4. Work harder to do constructive things about the negative features of the job (such as consider assertiveness training that might improve communications with management, try to think of more creative ways to handle paperwork and deal with inadequate resources, develop humorous anecdotes to lighten the tension, etc.).

5. Study avocational life away from the job to insure that there is adequate time being devoted to enjoyable activities that help to relieve tensions associated with the job.

6. Consider employment with another agency or a change in career. Keep in mind, however, that unless an elegant change is achieved with the irrational beliefs, these demands about the world could be an issue in any job. Also, the other homework assignments described above are important in other jobs.

GUIDELINES FOR DOING THE SWH

It is usually better to first identify the A = Activating Event and the C = Consequences (emotional and behavioral) and then identify the B = Beliefs. When the beliefs are identified, an indication can be placed in parentheses, after the emotion it is related to, as indicated in the example above. The client is also asked to really experience the inappropriate emotions. A caveat regarding responses to disputations is that a response made too rapidly may reflect more of a "memorized" answer. Many people in our culture know the rational answer but have never really thought it through and do not necessarily believe it. The client is also asked to really experience the appropriate emotions because they are an indication the process worked and are a powerful reinforcement.

Clients will vary in the amount of time it will take to do the above example of SWH. Although it is a brief therapeutic technique, even the most able client will want to take some time to do this assignment effectively. It is not so much the writing that takes time as dealing with the emotions and the thinking required. The final product will be enhanced by reflection that takes place over several solitary sessions. Less able clients will need more structure and concrete illustrations. Breaking it into parts and going over these parts in several therapy sessions with a counselor may also be helpful.

Some clients tend to view REBT as an authoritarian and aggressive approach (Gandy, 1992, 1995). Ellis (Ellis & Dryden, 1987) makes a distinction between "authoritarian" and "authoritative" and "aggressive" and "forceful." Authoritarian is dogmatically telling a person what to do, whereas authoritative is using expert knowledge and the scientific method to persuade a person. Aggressive is attacking the person, whereas forceful is attacking the irrational beliefs of the person but accepting the person. As indicated in Chapter 1, Ellis (Ellis & Dryden, 1987) indicates that there can be different therapeutic styles including less forceful styles, as long as one does not depart from the principles of REBT.

Even an "authoritative" and "forceful" approach is still threatening to some rehabilitation clients. A good compromise for such clients is the SWH technique. It is less threatening because they can do it in privacy by themselves. It is still a forceful approach because they are being asked to actively question and challenge themselves. The therapist can then later help to clarify or correct any aspect of their written homework.

Although the SWH can be used as a supplement to regular individual and/or group therapy sessions, it can also be used as a brief therapy stress management technique (Gandy, 1992, 1995; McGuigan, 1992). It can be used as one of those strategies for rational living that can be used to complement such techniques as progressive relaxation, systematic desensitization, biofeedback, and so forth.

ORGANIZATION OF CASE STUDIES

As indicated in the preface, the disputing of irrational beliefs within the SWH format will be applied to case examples of the mental health rehabilitation of individuals with mental and physical disabilities. Mental health rehabilitation is defined as therapeutic counseling designed to facilitate the emotional development of individuals with mental and physical disabilities that enables them to lead more productive lives. Productivity is considered to include avocational as well as vocational activities. The terms counseling and therapy are used interchangeably.

The remainder of this book, "Part Two: Case Studies," includes six chapters that provide case illustrations representing deafness, mood disorder, blindness, personality disorder, spinal cord injury, and substance abuse. As also noted in the preface, they represent a small sample of all possible disabilities. The purpose is to illustrate the disputing of irrational beliefs in the SWH format with representative major mental and physical disabilities. Although the cases are composites of various individuals, they are based on the author's experiences over the past twenty-five years. The cases are presented to emphasize educational, vocational, and avocational aspects, as well as personal and social concerns.

The following headings will be used in these case studies:

Statement of Problem and Background

Brief characteristics of the client such as age, marital status, family circumstances, disability, etc., and a concise statement of his or her problem are indicated in the first paragraph. The remainder of the section includes relevant social background information and a further development of the problem as it relates to the client's disability.

Counseling Assessment and Strategy

This section describes the early stages of the work of the counselor or therapist with the client. An assessment that includes placing the client's situation into an REBT framework is provided. Certain irrational beliefs are selected for the SWH technique.

Systematic Written Homework

A core irrational belief and at least two derivatives are illustrated in detail with the SWH technique. An effort was made to represent some typical irrational beliefs with certain disabilities, and all of the core irrational beliefs and derivatives based on the scheme presented in this chapter are represented:

> Chap. 4—Deafness—Beth—(Core iB: Demands about Self; Derivatives: Awfulizing and Damnation).
> Chap. 5—Mood Disorder—Karen (Core iB: Demands about Self; Derivatives: Damnation and I–Can't-Stand-it-itis).
> Chap. 6—Blindness—Susan (Core iB: Demands about Others; Derivatives: Awfulizing and I–Can't-Stand-it-itis).
> Chap. 7—Personality Disorder—Alan (Core iB: Demands about Others; Derivatives: Damnation and I–Can't-Stand-it-itis).
> Chap. 8—Spinal Cord Injury—Paul (Core iB: Demands about the World; Derivatives: Damnation and I–Can't-Stand-it-itis).
> Chap. 9—Substance Abuse—Michael (Core iB: Demands about the World; Derivatives: Awfulizing and Damnation).

Case Progress and Conclusion

The progress and outcome of the case after the SWH technique has been completed is described. Homework assignments are addressed as well as other relevant aspects. A conclusion with a focus on the future is provided.

REFERENCES

DiGiuseppe, R. (1991). Comprehensive cognitive disputing in RET. In M. E. Bernard (Ed.), *Using rational-emotive therapy effectively: A practitioner's guide.* New York: Plenum.

Ellis, A. (1971). *Growth through reason.* Palo Alto, CA: Science and Behavior Books.

Ellis, A. (1988). *How to stubbornly refuse to make yourself miserable about anything—yes anything!.* Secaucus, NJ: Lyle Stuart.

Ellis, A. (1989). Comments on my critics. In M. E. Bernard & R. DiGiuseppe (Eds.), *Inside rational-emotive therapy: A critical appraisal of the theory and therapy of Albert Ellis.* San Diego: Academic.

Ellis, A., & Dryden, W. (1987). *The practice of rational-emotive therapy.* New York: Springer.

Gandy, G. L. (1992, September). *Disputing irrational beliefs in rehabilitation counseling.* Paper presented at the Fourth International Conference on Stress Management, Paris, France.

Gandy, G. L. (1995). Disputing irrational beliefs in rehabilitation counseling. *Journal of Applied Rehabilitation Counseling, 26*(1), 36–40.

McGuigan, F. J. (1992). *Calm down: A guide for stress and tension control* (2nd ed.). Dubuque, Iowa: Kendall/Hunt.

Maultsby, M. C. (1971). Systematic written homework in psychotherapy. *Psychotherapy, 8,* 195–198.

Maultsby, M. C. (1974). Rational self-analysis (homework). In D. S. Goodman in collaboration with M. C. Maultsby, *Emotional well-being through rational behavior training.* Springfield, IL: Charles C Thomas.

Sichel, J., & Ellis, A. (1984). *RET self-help form.* New York: Institute for Rational-Emotive Therapy.

Walen, S. R., DiGiuseppe, R., and Dryden, W. (1992). *A practitioner's guide to rational-emotive therapy.* New York: Oxford.

Part Two
CASE STUDIES

Chapter 4

DEAFNESS—THE CASE OF BETH

STATEMENT OF PROBLEM AND BACKGROUND

Beth is 18 years old, unmarried, and has deafness as a result of an infectious disease as a child. She is in her first semester at a large state university away from home and is experiencing intense anxiety regarding her academic performance in school. Beth's father, age 43, is a unit manager for a department store; her mother, age 41, is a church secretary. She has a brother, two years younger, and a sister, three years younger. Her siblings do not have any major disabilities.

The family has basically experienced a comfortable middle class socio-economic status in a small community. Her parents initially experienced intense guilt feelings in regard to Beth's deafness and had difficulty accepting her deafness. They sought professional counseling and developed a more constructive perspective. Her parents and her siblings have been very supportive of Beth.

As a result of an infectious disease, cerebrospinal meningitis, at the age of five, Beth experienced permanent damage to the inner ear resulting in sensorineural deafness. Although she has some capacity for hearing sound, an evaluation determined that she would not benefit from hearing-aid equipment. She had been in good health prior to her illness and was not permanently injured in any other way. Her cognitive abilities were not affected, and her vision and larynx are normal. She recently had a physical examination that indicated she was in excellent health.

Beth had been a very capable child prior to the loss of her hearing. Her intelligence is considered to be in the superior range. She coped well with her disability by developing good speech skills, becoming exceptional at lipreading, and well skilled at both Ameslan (American Sign Language) and Manual English. She performed well in school, eventually graduating with honors (3.7 grade point average on a 4.0 system) from high school. Beth also developed a good social adjustment in school and community activities. She was particularly active with her church, a progressive Protestant denomination, and her own religious views are relatively moderate. She has an open-minded attitude about philosophical issues and values.

Although Beth is undecided about her future career, her success thus far would indicate that she has the potential to be successful in a university-educated profession. However, she is not doing well in her first semester of university study. Although the university has provided her with reasonable accommodations for her disability, the university environment is generally not as supportive of her disability as her home community, especially her family environment. Academic achievement at the university is far more competitive than at her high school. Her mid-term progress report indicates that, regardless of how well she performs the remainder of the semester, her overall academic achievement will be much lower than any previous school experience.

Beth is beginning to put pressure on herself about letting her family down. She is experiencing increased difficulty concentrating and accomplishing her homework assignments. She is suddenly fearful that she may have failing marks in some of her subjects by the end of the term. Her performance has been slightly above average in her psychology course, and she has been influenced by the material on therapeutic approaches and their effect on emotional states. After further discussing the situation with her roommate, who is not hearing impaired but is skilled in sign language, she became self-motivated to seek professional counseling at the university counseling center.

COUNSELING ASSESSMENT AND STRATEGY

The counselor observed that Beth was behind in her schoolwork and did not have very much time for counseling. Beth would also need to do something therapeutically very quickly if she were to have any impact on her academic performance for this semester. One alternative would be to request that she be allowed to withdraw from school in order to concentrate on counseling. The request could be based on the fact that her stress had been exacerbated by the disadvantage of her disability. She would have a withdrawal designation on her transcript but would avoid low and even possibly failing grades in some of her subjects. The disadvantages of this alternative were that it would be expensive in terms of lost tuition and place her a semester behind in progressing towards the completion of her degree.

Because of Beth's excellent academic ability and skills, good social adjustment history, and open-minded attitude, the counselor considered Beth an excellent candidate for brief therapy. Beth preferred not to have to withdraw from school and indicated that she would rather work toward the goal of improving her academic performance as much as possible. She was willing to accept the fact that, for this semester, her grades will probably be much lower than any previous school experience. If she could do something about her intense anxiety, she believed that she could avoid failing any subjects. Moreover, she thought she might be able to achieve at least "B" work in a couple of her subjects.

Beth was able to learn the principles of REBT very quickly. Her induction basically consisted of some short reading assignments and a couple of lecture/discussion sessions with a sign language interpreter available. After identifying the activating event as indicated above, she was able to get in touch with her emotions and describe them as primarily anxiety but also some depression and shame. Beth was soon able to identify her core irrational belief (core iB) as "I must excel academically at the university." She also identified two major derivatives: "It will be awful if I don't excel" and "I will be a worthless person if I don't excel." She was able to gain the insight that her emotions had primarily been created by these irrational beliefs.

With the help of her counselor, Beth also discovered that she was experiencing a secondary emotional disturbance. She was experiencing anxiety about anxiety primarily created by the beliefs that "I must not be anxious" and "I can't stand it." Before dealing with the primary emotional disturbance of anxiety, the counselor worked with her on the secondary emotional disturbance of anxiety about anxiety. She helped her to see that there was no reason why she shouldn't be anxious and that there was no evidence that she could not stand it.

Beth was able to overcome her secondary emotional disturbance very quickly; consequently, she and her counselor were able to focus on the primary problem. The counselor worked with her on putting her primary problem within the REBT framework. She taught her how to do the systematic written homework using a case example. Beth was assigned the systematic written homework task and reminded to first identify the activating event and the consequences and then identify the beliefs. She was able to complete the SWH with the help of her counselor within a few days. Her counselor helped her with a few minor changes in her disputations and cognitive effects. She also made some additional suggestions on her homework assignments. The final product is represented as follows:

SYSTEMATIC WRITTEN HOMEWORK—BETH

A. Not doing well in first semester of academic study:

   1. University community not as supportive of disability as home community, especially family environment.
   2. Academic achievement at the university is far more competitive than at high school.
   3. Regardless of performance remainder of semester, overall achievement will be much lower than previous experience.
   4. Failure of some courses is possible.

rB. 1. I want to excel academically at the university.
   2. It will be bad and uncomfortable if I don't excel at the university.
   3. I will not meet my standard if I don't excel at the university.

iB 1. I must excel academically at the university (Core iB).
   2. It will be awful if I don't excel at the university.
   3. I will be a worthless person if I don't excel.

C. Emotional:

   1. Intense anxiety related to iB # 1, # 2, & # 3.
   2. Mild depression related to iB # 2.
   3. Mild shame related to iB # 3.

   Behavioral:

   1. Difficulty concentrating on academic assignments.
   2. Underachievement in academic performance.

D. Disputing of iB # 1: I must excel academically at the university.

   D # 1 (logical dispute): Where is the logic that I must excel?
   cE # 1: Because I want to excel (which in itself is a matter of definition) does not mean that I will excel.
   D # 2 (empirical dispute): Where is the evidence that I must excel?
   cE # 2: My wanting to excel will motivate me and increase my probability of success but will not provide a guarantee.
   D # 3 (pragmatic dispute): How will holding the belief that I must excel help me to achieve my goal?

cE # 3: It is more likely to contribute to intense anxiety that will make it difficult for me to concentrate.

D # 4 (construction rational belief): What is an alternative belief that would better help me to excel?

cE # 4: I very much want to excel at the university and plan to work hard toward that goal. However, there is no guarantee that I will be successful. If I demand that I excel, I will lower, rather than increase, my probability of success.

eC of cE's of D's of iB # 1: intense concern about my academic performance at the university.

Disputing of iB # 2: It is awful if I don't excel at the university.

D # 1 (logical dispute): Where is the logic that it is awful if I don't excel?

cE # 1: I very much won't like it but that does not make it awful.

D # 2 (empirical dispute): Where is the evidence that it is awful if I don't excel?

cE # 2: It is bad and will cause me discomfort but is not awful.

D # 3 (pragmatic dispute): How will holding the belief that it is awful if I don't excel help me achieve my goal?

cE # 3: It will only depress me and decrease my energy level and motivation.

D # 4 (construction alternative belief): What is an alternative belief that would better help me to excel?

cE # 4: I will be unhappy with my performance if I don't excel, but it won't be awful. My energy level and motivation will be higher and increase my probability of a better performance if I maintain this more rational belief about my goal to excel.

eE of cE's of D's of iB # 2: intense concern and mild sadness about my performance.

Disputing of iB # 3: I will be a worthless person if I don't excel at the university.

D # 1 (logical dispute): Where is the logic that I will be a worthless person if I don't excel?

cE # 1: It does not logically follow that if I don't excel therefore I am a worthless person.

D # 2 (empirical dispute): Where is the evidence that I will be a worthless person if I don't excel?

cE # 2: The evidence is that if I don't excel I will only be a person who has not met my criteria of success for one aspect of my life.

D # 3 (pragmatic dispute): How will holding the belief that I am a worthless person if I don't excel help me achieve my goal?

cE # 3: It will cause me to take one aspect of my life to define my total being and make it seem like I am a failure to myself and in the eyes of my parents and other people.

D # 4 (construction rational belief): What is an alternative rational belief that would better help me to excel?

cE # 4: I am a person who places a value on high academic achievement. However, academic achievement is only one aspect of my behavior as a person and not my total essence. I want to work hard to achieve a realistic standard of performance for me but recognize that I may not always live up to my standard.

eE of cE's of D's of iB # 3: intense concern and mild disappointment about my performance.

bE. Homework Assignments:

1. Rational-Emotive Imagery (REI) and relaxation techniques.
The following assignments would better be accomplished after the completion of the semester.
2. Continued reading on REBT, especially material related to achievement.
3. Develop a clearer personal definition of "excel" and my ultimate goals in relation to that definition.
4. Visit the university career planning and placement center and begin work on identifying future career plans.
5. Seek a better social network support system at the university, perhaps in connection with the adjacent small community.

CASE PROGRESS AND CONCLUSION

Beth and her counselor agreed that brief Rational-Emotive Imagery (REI) and some brief relaxation exercises was the most she could accomplish in the remaining few weeks of the semester. The counselor helped her to structure these activities, and Beth concentrated on doing the best that she could with her academic work. She would begin the remainder of the assignments of self-help work after the completion of the semester.

Beth completed the semester with 3 C's and 2 B's, or a 2.4 grade point average on a 4.0 system. Considering that she had graduated with a 3.7 average from high school, she was very sad and disappointed about her performance. Receiving the grades was a shame-attacking exercise in itself. She was able to dispute and challenge and feel the sadness and disappointment rather than depression and shame. She was also very grateful that her grades were not as bad as she had thought they would be at one point and was highly motivated to perform better next semester.

The relaxation techniques had been very helpful, especially with test anxiety. Beth was also very pleased that the REI seemed to have had an impact on her overall perspective on academic achievement. She found that she could very effectively change her emotions from anxiety to concern about her performance. During the holiday period between the fall and spring semesters, she began reading material on REBT and achievement and giving thought to her own personal definition and ultimate goals.

After the beginning of the spring semester, Beth made an appointment at the university career planning and placement center. Her counselor at the university counseling center had suggested that it would probably help her with her concentration with her academic performance if she could become more focused in regard to her future career plans. With adaptations for her disability, she took some aptitude, vocational interest, and personality tests. Interpretation of results and career counseling helped her discover that she had the ability and interests, in spite of her disability, for occupations in the writing, teaching, and social service areas. She became very motivated to explore and gain further information about these areas in preparation for the decision on a major she would be required to make in her junior year.

With the help of her roommate, she began to explore possibilities of a better social network support system at the university in connection with the adjacent small community. Her roommate is not hearing impaired, but the disability is in her family, and she is skilled in sign language. Before long, they are able to develop a social network of people at the university and in the adjacent community who either have hearing disabilities, have relatives with hearing disabilities, or who have an interest in hearing disabilities.

Beth's academic performance was much improved. However, she decided before the end of the semester that she did not have to perform as well as she had in high school. In regard to her own personal definition of "excel," she wanted to make good enough grades to get into one of the professional occupational areas she was exploring, but she decided that it was unnecessary to attempt to match her performance in high school.

Rather than strive for achievement in itself, she decided to strive for achievement for her own satisfaction.

Beth's final grades for the semester involved 3 B's and 2 A's, or a 3.4 grade point average on a 4.0 system. Although she would have been delighted to make higher grades, she was very content with her performance. She had raised her overall grade point average to a 2.9 on a 4.0 system. According to the information she had obtained on the occupational areas of interest to her, she was now eligible, in terms of grade point average, to enter an undergraduate major in one of those areas. It was also realistic to assume that she could raise her grade point average sufficiently to become an excellent candidate for graduate study that included financial support.

Beth made a few visits to her counselor at the University Counseling Center during the spring semester. Her counselor helped her with some of her homework assignments but primarily encouraged her to be her own therapist. Beth began to generalize her learning about her "need to excel" to other areas of her life and developed more of an abstract rational belief about achievement in general. She also developed the understanding that she had experienced what in REBT would be considered an ego disturbance. By the beginning of the next fall semester, Beth concluded that she had experienced an elegant change in regard to her previous ego disturbance "need to excel." However, when she discovered some of the requirements in her courses for the fall semester, she experienced some anger. She thought to herself, "What am I telling myself?" Her answer was, "It shouldn't be this hard." She turned on her computer and began doing systematic written homework on her discomfort disturbance.

Chapter 5

MOOD DISORDER—THE CASE OF KAREN

STATEMENT OF PROBLEM AND BACKGROUND

Karen is 24 years old, divorced, no children, and has recently been diagnosed as having a major depressive disorder, single episode. She has worked as a waitress, a food counter attendant, and a fast-food worker during the past six years. She is currently unemployed and subsisting on welfare payments.

Karen was 18 and recently graduated from high school when she met Bill, who was 20. She was a waitress at a restaurant, and he was a student at a nearby large state university. They decided to get married after dating for only a few months. While Karen worked at the various positions described above, Bill's parents were able to help him with school expenses through his bachelor's degree. Bill was able to obtain a graduate assistantship and some scholarship money when he entered graduate school.

Bill is currently in a doctoral program. However, after completing his master's degree, he surprised Karen with the desire to be divorced. He noted that they had always been incompatible intellectually and now there was a significant educational difference. He felt that their main attraction had been physical and that they had both had loneliness needs.

Bill and Karen separated after over four years of marriage and were divorced the following year. Karen agreed to a no-fault divorce and did not receive alimony. They divided their personal possessions and their limited monetary savings. Karen moved to a boarding house near her mother and continued to work as a fast-food worker. Eventually, she lost her job because of tardiness and unexcused absences from work.

A primary care physician obtained a psychiatric consultation, and Karen was diagnosed as having a major depressive reaction, single episode. She had been depressed and unable to concentrate for three months since the divorce. She had lost weight and had difficulty sleeping. She

45

expressed strong feelings of worthlessness and some suicidal ideation. Karen had some of these symptoms during the year of separation but not on a consistent basis. She had hoped for a reconciliation with Bill, but she gave up hope after the divorce was final.

Karen is an only child, and she lost her father when she was 10 years old. He was a construction worker and was killed in an accident at work when he was 31 years old. The psychiatric consultation suggested that this event had made Karen more vulnerable to depressive illness. Also, there was some history of depression on her mother's side of the family. Her mother, who is currently 42 years old, has continued to work as a homemaker—home health aide. She and her mother have always been close, but her mother has been somewhat overly emotionally protective of Karen.

Karen's records in high school indicate that she has average intelligence and that her grades were consistently average. Although most would consider her to be somewhat more physically attractive than the average person, she did not date very often and was not very active in social activities. She had attended church occasionally to please her mother but had not been significantly influenced by a religious orientation. She did not read very much but enjoyed television and movies.

Antidepressant medication helped Karen's symptoms. However, the primary care physician and the psychiatric consultant both agreed that Karen would benefit from some form of professional counseling/therapy. She was referred to a community center that included counseling, social, and rehabilitation service activities.

COUNSELING ASSESSMENT AND STRATEGY

Karen was very uncomfortable during the first few sessions with her therapist. She did not understand counseling and was apprehensive about what to expect. He sensed Karen's discomfort and took more time than he normally would have to help her feel at ease and provide some structure to the counseling process. She eventually became more comfortable with the experience and began to share her thoughts and feelings. The therapist was very careful not only to empathize with Karen's situation but also to convey this sense of empathy to Karen.

Because Karen's intelligence was more in the average range and she was not particularly academically oriented, the therapist described a number of concrete examples and illustrations of the REBT process. He provided her with audiotape recordings of their sessions and audiotapes describing or explaining various aspects of REBT. He also loaned her a videotape that had been developed at the counseling center to better illustrate REBT in a concrete manner. The reading material he provided her with was brief and very basic.

The therapist was initially more indirect in helping Karen uncover and dispute her irrational beliefs. For example, after Karen began to understand REBT, she was able to pick out many of her irrational thoughts and inappropriate emotions by listening to the audiotaped recordings of her sessions. He then gave her the homework assignment of audiotape recording the advice she would give a good friend with such feelings and thoughts. He went over these recordings with her and also had her role play, using two chairs, the conflict between rational and irrational beliefs.

Karen's irrational beliefs regarding her divorce from Bill were: "I should have been able to make my marriage work" (core iB), "I am a failure and a worthless person because my marriage didn't work" (1st derivative), and "I can't stand it that I could not make my marriage work" (2nd derivative). Her pervasive emotional reaction is depression, but she is also experiencing guilt, shame, and anger. The emotional reactions were also contributing to a secondary emotional reaction of depression created by the belief that "I must not have these feelings," and "I must truly be a worthless person if I have these feelings."

Karen's therapist took a lot of time with her on the secondary emotional disturbance, and she was eventually able to see that it was a normal reaction and there was no reason why she shouldn't have these feelings. They also made a lot of progress on the primary emotional disturbance. He was able to get her involved in group work at the community center with women who were divorced and had similar self-esteem issues. Her affect improved and she seemed to have more energy.

The therapist discussed the possibility of systematic written homework with Karen. He suggested that by writing the material down she could confront herself even more strongly and deepen her convictions in her rational beliefs. With his help, it would also be good for her to outline some future homework assignments that would impact on her future life upon the completion of counseling. Karen indicated that she was interested in doing the systematic written homework.

As he did when he initially explained the REBT process, the therapist used a lot of concrete examples and illustrations to explain the systematic written homework process to Karen. He also had her do the process in steps rather than all at once. For example, he first had her write out the activating event and the emotional and behavioral consequences, and he went over these with her in the next session. She then completed the rational beliefs and irrational beliefs. Next she did the disputations, cognitive effects, and emotive effects. Finally, they worked on the homework assignments together. Her final product is represented below:

SYSTEMATIC WRITTEN HOMEWORK—KAREN

A. Divorce from husband.

    1. No children after over 5 years of marriage.

    2. Husband considered me to be intellectually and educationally inferior.

    3. Agreed to a no fault divorce; did not think I deserved any special compensation.

    4. Viewed by others as a failure.

rB.   1. I wanted to make my marriage work.

    2. I have made a mistake with my marriage.

    3. I don't like it that I could not make my marriage work.

iB.   1. I should have been able to make my marriage work (Core iB).

    2. I am a failure and a worthless person because my marriage didn't work.

    3. I can't stand it that I could not make my marriage work.

C. Emotional:

    1. Intense depression related to iB # 1, 2, & 3.

    2. Intense guilt related to iB # 1.

    3. Intense shame related to iB # 2.

    4. Intense anger related to iB # 3.

Behavioral:

    1. Dismissed from job because of tardiness and unexcused absences.

    2. Unable to concentrate, loss of weight, and difficulty sleeping.

D. Disputing of iB # 1: I should have been able to make my marriage work.

D # 1 (logical dispute): Where is the logic that I should have been able to make it work?

cE # 1: The fact that I wanted it to work does not mean that it would have worked.

D # 2 (empirical dispute): Where is the evidence that I should have been able to make it work?

cE # 2: My desire helps but there is no evidence that desire will insure that a marriage will work.

D # 3 (pragmatic dispute): How will holding the belief that I should have made it work help me in the future?

cE # 3: It will more likely contribute to intense depression and guilt that will immobilize me and keep me from going on with my life.

D # 4 (construction rational belief): What is an alternative belief that would better help me with future goals?

cE # 4: I would have liked for my marriage to have worked. However, desire will not always bring me what I want. It would be better for me to now focus on the future.

eE of cE's of D's of iB # 1: Intense sadness and regret about the fact that, in spite of my efforts, my marriage did not work.

Disputing of irrational belief # 2: I am a failure and a worthless person because my marriage did not work.

D # 1 (logical dispute): Where is the logic that I am a failure and a worthless person?

cE # 1: My marriage did not work but that does not make me a failure or a worthless person.

D # 2 (empirical dispute): Where is the evidence that I am a failure or a worthless person?

cE # 2: The evidence is that I am a person who made a mistake in regard to my marriage and some other things but have not made mistakes about everything in my life.

D # 3 (pragmatic dispute): How will holding the belief that I am a failure and a worthless person help me with future goals?

C # 3: It will contribute to feelings of shame and depression, which will make it difficult for me to concentrate on developing behaviors and activities that are worthwhile and successful.

D # 4 (construction rational belief): What is an alternative rational belief that would better help me with future goals?

cE # 4: I made a mistake in regard to my marriage, but I have not made a mistake about everything in my life. Moreover, I can choose to focus on developing future behaviors and activities that are worthwhile and successful.

eE of cE's of D's of iB # 2: Intense sadness and sorrow about the mistake I made with my marriage.

Disputing of iB # 3: I can't stand it that I could not make my marriage work.

D # 1 (logical dispute): Where is the logic that I can't stand it?

cE # 1: Just because I think I can't stand it that I could not make my marriage work does not make it so.

D # 2 (empirical dispute): Where is the evidence that I can't stand it?

cE # 2: The evidence is that it is very painful for me that I could not make my marriage work, but that does not prove that I can't stand it.

D # 3 (pragmatic dispute): How will holding the belief that I can't stand it help with future goals?

cE # 3: It will only contribute to depression that will make it difficult for me to accept the fact that I could not make my marriage work.

D # 4: (construction rational belief): What is an alternative belief that would better help me with my future goals?

cE # 4: I can stand it that I could not make my marriage work. It is very painful, but I can accept what I cannot change and go on with my life.

eE of cE's of D's of iB # 3: Intense sadness and disappointment that my marriage did not work.

bE. Homework Assignments:

1. Apply REBT to other irrational beliefs.
2. Continue to participate in group work with women who are divorced and have similar self-esteem issues.
3. Explore free or low-cost social and recreational activities in the community.
4. Actively participate in work evaluation and work adjustment program through community rehabilitation services.

CASE PROGRESS AND CONCLUSION

Due to the fact that Karen's intellectual functioning was more at a concrete level, she was not able to generalize her learning very well to similar ego disturbance issues. However, she did understand the REBT process and, with the help of her therapist, was able to apply the principles to such irrational beliefs. For example, she successfully applied the systematic written homework technique to the irrational belief, "I should have been able to marry the right person for me in the beginning."

Karen continued her participation in the group work with women who were divorced and had similar self-esteem issues. They all agreed to try some risk-taking and shame-attacking homework exercises and share their experiences with the group. The exercises were designed to desensitize them to a fear of failure and to distinguish between their behavior and their worth as a human being. They learned to rate their behavior and not themselves. These concrete and practical exercises were very helpful to Karen in terms of her self-esteem. The group also focused on developing a better sense of humor by being able to laugh at their behavior at times but not themselves. The latter was useful to Karen in helping her to not take things so seriously.

Karen began to do very well with self-esteem issues; however, she soon developed some discomfort disturbances. For example, she soon found herself feeling angry and hurt toward her former husband ("he shouldn't have been the way he was"; "damn him for treating me the way he did"). She also developed the irrational belief that "she did not deserve to have to put up with this kind of hassle in life."

Karen's therapist helped her to realize that it was normal for other irrational beliefs to develop. Her focus had been on self-esteem issues, and she had not even thought about these other issues. However, as she developed a better acceptance of herself, she became more aware of her former husband's inconsiderateness and the fact that life is often unfair. She was able to apply the REBT principles to these irrational beliefs and develop a better perspective on discomfort issues.

With the help of a social worker at the community center, Karen began to explore free or low-cost social and recreational activities in the community. She soon found herself participating in a women's group involved with exercise and physical appearance. Her work with this group not only improved her physical appearance but enhanced her general mental attitude. She was eventually participating in social activities that focused more on interpersonal interactions.

During the time she was engaged in all of the above activities, Karen was also participating in the community rehabilitation services work evaluation and work adjustment program. Evaluation indicated that with her improved mental state, she could probably return to work that was related to her previous employment. However, the evaluation also indicated that she was eligible for a variety of community-sponsored training programs. She eventually elected to enroll in a secretarial training program at a vocational training center.

Karen's evaluation and therapeutic work through the community center covered a period of approximately one year. She then began an eighteen-month secretarial training program. She continued with the social and recreational contacts that she had been able to establish through the center. After completing her secretarial training program, she was employed by a medical supply company as a receptionist and secretary. Three years after her initial visit to the community center, she was engaged to an emergency medical technician at a nearby hospital.

Chapter 6

BLINDNESS—THE CASE OF SUSAN

STATEMENT OF PROBLEM AND BACKGROUND

Susan is 45 years old and is married to John who is 47 years old. They have been married 27 years and have three children, a daughter, 18, and two sons, 23 and 25. Susan was diagnosed about six months ago as having primary glaucoma, chronic open-angle type, and is considered legally blind. Severe impairment was present before the disease was detected. The nerve fibers were damaged and the impairment is irreversible. The disability has had a devastating effect on Susan and her family.

Susan was primarily a homemaker much of her adult life. However, as her children got older, she began to help John with the development of his furniture business. She was primarily involved with the business office activities such as bookkeeping, typing, filing, etc. Her daughter has just finished a high school business-secretarial curriculum and has been able to take over these functions temporarily. Susan and John's oldest son, who is engaged to be married, works with his father in the business. The youngest son is a carpenter who works as his own contractor on small jobs, occasionally doing work for his father or his customers.

All of the children are currently making sacrifices in regard to their own personal priorities in order to help their mother cope with the impact of her disability. The oldest son has taken on more responsibility with the business and postponed his marital plans in order to give his father more time with his mother. The daughter is taking care of the business office aspects and helping her mother as a caretaker at home, although she would eventually prefer a job and living accommodations independent of her family. The youngest son helps with various errands and projects, passing up contractual work that might interfere with his availability.

Susan's educational background involves a general high school diploma. She was a good student, and her high school guidance counselor thought she could have completed a college preparatory curriculum. Intelligence tests had indicated that she was above average for the general population and slightly into the range of college preparatory students. Susan's parents did not have the financial resources to send her to college. Susan developed other interests, taking courses in home economics and various business subjects. She was married at 18, immediately upon graduation from high school.

With the exception of her contact with her immediate family, Susan has for the most part become socially withdrawn since the onset of her disability. She initially made some attempts to make contact with other people but had some embarrassing experiences and did not make further efforts. She has resisted taking advantage of services at the Rehabilitation Center for Visual Disabilities. Although John brought her some literature on assistive technology for visual impairments, she has not bothered to read it.

Susan has met with her minister a few times, although she has advised him that she doesn't feel like attending church at the present time. Susan and John are members of a relatively moderate Protestant denomination. Their minister has had pastoral counseling training as part of his professional education. He now has a number of years of experience as a parish minister. Susan has a lot of trust and confidence in her minister.

After meeting with her several times, Susan's minister confronted her with the possibility that she might be able to make a better adjustment to her disability. He pointed out that she may have the potential to become more independent of her family and that it might be better for her and them. He noted that a first step would be to deal with some emotions and thoughts that were not helpful to her adjustment. He recommended that she make an appointment with a private pastoral group involved with full-time professional counseling.

COUNSELING ASSESSMENT AND STRATEGY

After giving it some thought, Susan decided to follow up on her minister's recommendation. She met with a female counselor who initially helped her to explore her feelings. Susan talked about the depression she had experienced as a result of the advent of her disability. She had also had to deal with some guilt about the fact that she might have been better with her medical examinations, which might have helped to prevent some of the effects of the glaucoma.

More recently, Susan indicated that she was experiencing resentment and anger toward other people who, even when their intention was well meaning, tended to be patronizing and insensitive. She described her first experience in a restaurant after losing her sight as humiliating and degrading. The waitress asked John what Susan wanted from the menu rather than directly addressing her. Even friends and acquaintances tended to act awkward by saying things that sounded more like pity than compassion.

Susan's husband and children seemed to be very sensitive to her feelings about her experiences in public and with other people. She is very close to her family and did not interpret any of their behavior to be comparable to other people. However, she was unaware of the fact that a lot of their behavior was a related problem. They were working very hard to protect her but were encouraging her to be more insulated and dependent.

Susan accepted the idea of using a tape recorder and began to listen to tapes of her therapy sessions. After explaining the principles and describing examples of REBT, the therapist provided other tapes about REBT to Susan. With the help of her therapist, Susan was able to put her initial depression and guilt about her disability into the REBT framework. She realized that she had already worked through much of these issues, but the REBT process helped bring more resolution. She was now experiencing intense sadness and regret but accepting the reality of the situation.

Her acceptance of her disability also helped Susan to develop a different perspective about herself in spite of the patronizing behavior of other people. She developed the realization that she didn't have to put herself down because of their behavior. She began to feel sorrow rather than shame about the fact that she was a person with an obvious visual disability. However, she continued to feel angry and somewhat depressed about the behavior of other people. Susan's therapist helped her to identify her irrational beliefs about other people as: "Other people shouldn't be so insensitive about blindness" (core iB), "It is awful that other people are so insensitive about blindness" (1st derivative), and "I can't stand it that other people are so insensitive about blindness" (2nd derivative).

Susan's therapist helped her to realize that she was not using her own acceptance of her disability and herself very effectively in regard to other people. Because Susan was able to accept her disability and herself, she was demanding that other people be able to accomplish the same thing. Susan admitted that her acceptance of her disability and herself could contribute to others better developing a better perspective about her and her disability but could not guarantee it.

Susan was very receptive to putting her irrational beliefs about other people into the form of systematic written homework (first identifying the activating event and the emotional and behavioral consequences). She had become comfortable with using the tape recorder, and her daughter was very willing to type her assignment out so that Susan's therapist could more easily go over it with her. Susan did very well on her first effort, and her therapist helped her to elaborate on her homework assignments. Susan's systematic written homework is represented as follows:

SYSTEMATIC WRITTEN HOMEWORK—SUSAN

A. **Insensitivity by other people toward blindness.**

  1. **Patronizing comments**
  2. **Pitying attitude**
  3. **Awkward behavior**

rB. 1. It would be nice if other people were more sensitive about blindness.
  2. It is unpleasant when people are insensitive about blindness.
  3. I don't like it when people are insensitive about blindness.

iB. 1. Other people shouldn't be so insensitive about blindness (core iB).
  2. It is awful when other people are so insensitive about blindness.
  3. I can't stand it when other people are so insensitive about blindness.

C. **Emotional:**

  1. **Intense anger and resentment related to iB # 1, 2, & 3.**
  2. **Mild depression related to iB # 3.**
  Behavioral:
  1. **Social withdrawal from people.**

D. **Disputing of iB # 1: Other people shouldn't be so insensitive about blindness.**

  D # 1 (logical dispute): Where is the logic that people shouldn't be so insensitive?

  cE # 1: The fact that I can and have accepted myself and my

disability does not mean that other people will or can do the same thing.

D # 2 (empirical dispute): Where is the empirical evidence that other people shouldn't be so insensitive?

cE # 2: My own acceptance will increase the probability that other people will be more sensitive, but that doesn't ensure that it will happen.

D # 3 (pragmatic belief): How will holding the belief that other people shouldn't be so insensitive help me with my adjustment?

cE # 3: It will make it difficult for me to be motivated to be active and involved with other people who do not experience blindness.

D # 4 (construction rational belief): What is an alternative belief that would better help me with my adjustment?

cE # 4: It would be helpful if other people were more sensitive about blindness but that very often is not the case. The fact that I can accept myself and my disability may help contribute to more sensitivity on their part.

eE of cE's of D's of iB # 1: Intense anger at people's insensitive behavior but not at their person.

Disputing of irrational belief # 2: It is awful when other people are so insensitive about blindness.

D # 1 (logical dispute): Where is the logic that it is awful when other people are so insensitive?

cE # 1: It is unfortunate when other people are so insensitive but that does not make it awful.

D # 2 (empirical dispute): Where is the evidence that it is awful when people are so insensitive?

cE # 2: It is very unpleasant when people are so insensitive but that is not the same as awful.

D # 3 (pragmatic dispute): How will holding the belief that it is awful when other people are so insensitive help me with my adjustment?

cE # 3: It will make me angry and cause me to withdraw from other people.

D # 4: (construction rational belief): What is an alternative belief that would better help me with my adjustment?

cE # 4: It is unfortunate when other people are so insensitive about blindness because it is very unpleasant. All I can do is work toward a constructive impact on such behavior.

eE of cE's of D's of iB # 2: Intense disappointment about the fact that people display such insensitive behavior.

Disputing of irrational belief # 3: I can't stand it when other people are so insensitive about blindness.

D # 1 (logical dispute): Where is the logic that I can't stand it when other people are so insensitive?

cE # 1: I very much don't like it when other people are so insensitive but that doesn't mean I can't stand it.

D # 2 (empirical dispute): Where is the evidence that I can't stand it when other people are so insensitive?

cE # 2: It is very unpleasant for me when other people are so insensitive but I can stand it.

D # 3 (pragmatic dispute): How will holding the belief that I can't stand it when other people are so insensitive help me with my adjustment?

cE # 3: It will probably cause me to be angry and depressed and prevent me from having the energy to do anything about it.

D # 4 (construction rational belief): What is an alternative belief that would better help me with my adjustment?

cE # 4: I don't like it when other people are so insensitive about blindness, and it is very unpleasant for me. However, I can stand it and can do my best to do something about it.

eE of cE's of D's of iB # 3: Intense frustration and sadness that such insensitive behavior from other people is a reality.

bE. Homework Assignments:

1. Participate in the rehabilitation program at the Community Center for Visual Disabilities.
2. Consider becoming involved again with her social support network external to her immediate family.
3. Continue her study of REBT and begin to generalize her learning, especially as it relates to disability issues and personal independence.

CASE PROGRESS AND CONCLUSION

With the help of professional counseling and the systematic written homework procedure, Susan made considerable progress in regard to adjustment to her disability, as well as acceptance of the behavior of other people. She became motivated to become involved with the rehabilitation program at the Community Center for Visual Disabilities. She was amazed at how such features as orientation and mobility training, techniques of social and personal functioning, and the use of assistive technology could be so helpful in enabling her to be more independent.

With the visual disability rehabilitation she was receiving at the Community Center, Susan became more encouraged about involving herself again with her social network system external to her family. Nevertheless, she experienced some apprehension and anxiety about risking her self-esteem in this way. However, she continued her study of REBT, mechanically made easier now by the use of assistive technology. She was able to check out books and articles from the pastoral counseling center. She began to generalize her learning to other irrational beliefs such as "I shouldn't make a fool of myself in front of my friends" and "I can't stand it if my friends reject me."

Another factor that motivated Susan to involve herself again socially was she developed the realization that she had become too dependent on her family. Susan recognized that she was fortunate to have a caring and concerned family. However, it occurred to her that it was unfair to depend so much on them when she has the potential to do more for herself physically and socially. Her therapist helped her to realize that her dependency and her family's overprotectiveness was a normal reaction. It was now time to move forward from this stage. She began to attend church activities again and to involve herself in many of her previous social activities.

Susan's return to social involvement was not without frustration as well as a reoccurrence of some of her previous inappropriate emotions and irrational beliefs. However, she soon found that this involvement was helping her to make a truly elegant philosophical change in regard to her irrational beliefs. Moreover, Susan began to see, in a more practical way, how emotions such as intense anger at people's acts, disappointment, frustration, and sadness were very motivating and more constructive than emotions such as anger at the person and depression.

Experiencing appropriate emotions and rational beliefs, Susan soon found that she could have a personal social impact on other people. She found that she could work harder to educate them about visual disability in informal ways by providing social cues, or more directly, by politely informing them. She had also made friends in the visual disability community, and her social network involved a combination of some of her previous social contacts as well as new contacts.

Susan's physical and social rehabilitation was having a very positive impact on her family. Her husband was able to resume most of his previous responsibilities with his furniture business. Her oldest son and his fiancee have set a wedding date. The youngest son no longer has to pass up desirable carpentry contracts. The daughter is still helping out with the business office activities, but she is now relieved of major caretaker activities at home and is able to resume her social life.

So that their daughter can pursue her own career independently of the family or perhaps be in a position to start her own family, Susan's husband has indicated a willingness to hire a full-time administrative assistant. However, Susan is considering the possibility of returning to that role with the help of a part-time clerical assistant and assistive technology, such as a voice-activated computer.

Chapter 7

PERSONALITY DISORDER—THE CASE OF ALAN

STATEMENT OF PROBLEM AND BACKGROUND

Alan is 32 years old, twice divorced, and has one son, three years old, who lives with his second ex-wife. He has been diagnosed as having a narcissistic personality disorder with associated features of a borderline personality disorder. He has a bachelor's degree in business management but is currently underemployed as a supply clerk in a warehouse. He recently voluntarily sought therapy at a community mental health center because of many difficulties he has experienced in his personal and occupational life over a period of years.

Alan is the oldest of two children. He has one brother four years younger who is a certified public accountant. He has always been envious of his younger brother and competitive with him. His father has been a pharmaceutical representative for many years, and his mother is a homemaker. His parents admit they made mistakes in raising him, which they were able to correct with the second child. They were overly indulgent and helped him to create unrealistic expectations about life. Alan has a grandiose sense of self-importance that makes him feel he is destined for unusual success.

Alan was an overall B student in high school, but his grades were variable. His high school guidance counselor had suggested to his parents that he frequently performed below his potential. Intelligence test scores did not indicate that he was unusually gifted, but they did suggest that he was very bright. He was admitted to a large state university where he made average grades and graduated with a bachelor's degree in business management.

For the past ten years, Alan's personal and occupational life has been very unstable. He was married upon graduation from the university and, at the same time, entered a good management training program with a national hotel chain. He soon encountered difficulty in his work because of arrogant and haughty behavior. He began to have difficulty in his marriage because of what his wife described as a lack of sensitivity to her feelings. She felt he was more preoccupied with his own needs and interests. Within a couple of years, he was separated from his wife (eventually divorced) and had lost his position with the national hotel chain.

Alan felt that he had married the wrong person, and he concluded that he should be working for himself rather than an organization. He borrowed money from his friends and his family in order to start his own business. However, the business failed within a year mainly because of his grandiose ideas and schemes, and he never paid the money back. He held several business supervisory positions for small organizations over the next few years. His superficial charm and grace would help in initially getting these positions, but he would eventually clash with either his co-workers, customers, or his immediate supervisors and either resign or be asked to leave.

When he was employed in his last supervisory position, he met and soon married his second wife. They had a son together within the first year of marriage. However, they had already begun to experience difficulties. She complained about his lack of empathy and moody behavior. He went with her for marriage counseling for awhile but finally decided that he wanted to get out of this situation. After his divorce, he lost his last supervisory position. He began to experience difficulty obtaining employment and managed to obtain unemployment compensation a few times.

Alan was recently employed as a supply clerk in an industrial products warehouse. It is a steady position and he is able to meet his basic financial needs. However, he is underemployed in relation to his education and ability and is living at a lower socioeconomic level than he ever envisioned. Moreover, his difficulties with his former wives, family, and friends have prompted him to decide that professional counseling would be of benefit to him. He feels he needs some help in getting other people to behave in a better way towards him. He is able to arrange therapeutic treatment at a community mental health center at a fee commensurate with his income.

COUNSELING ASSESSMENT AND STRATEGY

Alan had done some reading over the years in the area of traditional psychoanalysis. He thought he would be able to save his therapist some time by providing him with a well-thought-out framework on his background. From Alan's perspective, his problems had been brought about by the way his parents had raised him. He perceived the goal of therapy as helping him to work through some emotional issues in regard to his parents. Once he was able to come to terms with these issues, he thought he would then be able to better deal with the problems of other people who didn't seem to understand him or appreciate his special and unique personality.

Alan's therapist initially worked with him in consultation with a clinical psychologist on the staff of the mental health center who has an expertise in clinical personality assessment. Alan's therapist and the colleague both agreed that Alan was demonstrating the characteristics of a narcissistic personality disorder with associated features of a borderline personality disorder as defined in the *Diagnostic and Statistical Manual of Mental Disorders (DSM-IV)*, Fourth Edition. The diagnosis was helpful, but Alan's therapist recognizes the limitations of a categorical classification as is addressed in the *DSM-IV*.

Although Alan's therapist planned to use a lot of Rational Emotive Behavior Therapy with him, he also recognized a limitation of this approach with someone displaying some of Alan's characteristics. Alan is very bright which, when combined with his tendency to rationalize, makes it easier for him to twist and distort a cognitive-behavioral approach. These characteristics also make it harder to get in touch with feelings. When confronted in a cognitive way, Alan tends to intellectualize rather than relate it to his feelings.

Because of Alan's tendency to rationalize and intellectualize, his therapist initially used expressive-emotive-experiential Gestalt procedures with him. He had Alan perform a lot of fantasy and role-playing exercises, especially assuming the roles of his parents as well as interactions with them. He helped Alan bring the past to the present, begin to use language that assumed more responsibility for self (e.g., "I" rather than "you") and become more aware of nonverbal behavior.

His therapist also capitalized on Alan's extensive reading of traditional psychoanalysis material. He helped Alan put psychoanalytic concepts into more of a social-psychological perspective. He particularly focused on defense mechanisms, such as projection, rationalization, denial, and reaction formation, and was able to get Alan to identify this behavior in himself as well as in other people.

Eventually, his therapist began to help Alan put his issues into a

Rational Emotive Behavior Therapy perspective. He helped Alan identify the irrational beliefs, "The world should be the way I want it to be," "Damn the world for not being the way I want it to be," and "I can't stand the world being this way." He began to help Alan recognize some of his grandiosity and arrogance. Alan demonstrated a lot of insight in regard to pragmatic disputes about how these beliefs were not helping him achieve his goals.

Alan had more difficulty in relating REBT principles to his thoughts and feelings about other people, especially those close to him such as former spouses, family, and friends. His therapist worked with him in regard to specific individuals and events. He particularly focused on Alan's sense of entitlement and interpersonal exploitative behavior. They then decided to try the systematic written homework procedure, defining the activating event as an abstract generalization about how others don't often enough do what he wants them to do.

Alan's therapist helped him get in touch with the emotions of anger and depression. They then identified the irrational beliefs of: "Others should do what I want them to do" (core iB), "Damn others for not doing what I want them to do" (1st derivative), and "I can't stand it when others don't do what I want them to do" (2nd derivative). His therapist had to help Alan with some revisions because he tended to revert to his previous pattern of rationalizing. His therapist also made some major suggestions on homework assignments, especially in terms of his accuracy of perception of the activating event. The final product is represented below.

SYSTEMATIC WRITTEN HOMEWORK—ALAN

A. **Others don't do what I want them to do often enough, as reflected by the following examples:**

   1. **Don't give me enough attention.**
   2. **Don't give me enough recognition.**
   3. **Don't give me enough resources.**
   4. **Don't forgive me for my mistakes.**
   5. **Don't try to understand my uniqueness.**

rB. 1. **It is desirable that other people often do what I want them to do.**
   2. **Other people are exhibiting dissatisfying behavior when they don't do often what I want them to do.**

3. I don't like it when other people don't often do what I want them to do.

iB. 1. Other people should often do what I want them to do (Core iB).
2. Damn other people when they don't often do what I want them to do.
3. I can't stand it when other people don't often do what I want them to do.

C. Emotional:

1. Intense anger related to iB # 1, 2, & 3.
2. Intense depression related to iB # 3.

Behavioral:

1. Unstable interpersonal relationships.

D. Disputing of irrational belief # 1: Other people should often do what I want them to do.

D # 1 (logical dispute): Where is the logic that other people should often do what I want them to do?

cE # 1: It does not logically follow that because I want people to often do what I want that they will do it.

D # 2 (empirical dispute): Where is the evidence that other people should often do what I want them to do?

cE # 2: The evidence is that other people often do what they want to do.

D # 3 (pragmatic dispute): How will holding the belief that other people should often do what I want them to do help me to achieve my goals?

cE # 3: It will cause me to waste time and energy because it is an unrealistic expectation.

D # 4 (construction rational belief): What is an alternative belief that will better help me achieve my goals?

cE # 4: It is nice when people often do what I want them to do, but they are often going to do what they want to do. I can use my time and energy more efficiently if I have a more realistic expectation of their behavior.

eC of cE's of D's of iB # 1: Intense disappointment about the fact that people don't often do what I want them to do.

Disputing of irrational belief # 2: Damn other people for not often doing what I want them to do.

D # 1 (logical dispute): Where is the logic that other people should be damned for not often doing what I want them to do?

cE # 1: Just because I am dissatisfied with other people's behavior does not mean that I should damn the people.

D # 2 (empirical dispute): Where is the evidence that other people should be damned for not often doing what I want them to do?

cE # 2: The evidence is that there are no good or bad people but only people who do good and bad things.

D # 3 (pragmatic dispute): How will holding the belief that other people should be damned for not often doing what I want them to do help me achieve my goals?

cE # 3: It will not be helpful because it will cause me to have inappropriate anger toward their person, which will probably create major interpersonal difficulties.

D # 4 (construction rational belief): What is an alternative belief that will better help me achieve my goals?

cE # 4: I am dissatisfied with other people's behavior when they don't often do what I want them to do, but people's behavior is not the same as their person.

eE of cE's of D's of iB # 2: intense frustration about people's behavior.

Disputing of iB # 3: I can't stand it when other people don't often do what I want them to do.

D # 1 (logical dispute): Where is the logic that I can't stand it when other people don't often do what I want them to do?

cE # 1: The only reason I can't stand it is because I'm telling myself I can't stand it.

D # 2 (empirical dispute): Where is the evidence that I can't stand it when other people don't often do what I want them to do?

cE # 2: The evidence is that it makes me very uncomfortable but it won't kill me.

D # 3 (pragmatic dispute): How will holding the belief that I can't stand it when other people don't often do what I want them to do help me to achieve my goals?

cE # 3: It will not be helpful because it will cause me to focus too much on what I am unhappy about with other people.

D # 4 (construction rational belief): What is an alternative belief that would better help me to achieve my goals?

cE # 4: I don't like it when other people don't often do what I want them to do. It is very uncomfortable, but I can stand it.

eE of cE's of D's of iB # 3: Intense disappointment and sadness about the fact that people don't often do what I want them to do.

bE. Homework Assignments:

1. Explore the accuracy of my perception of the activating event.
2. Participate in group therapy that involves a combination of expressive-emotive-experiential Gestalt procedures and Rational Emotive Behavior Therapy.
3. Become involved in a social group involving new friends and acquaintances and practice the principles of intrapersonal and interpersonal functioning that I have learned in my therapeutic experiences.
4. Assess what occupational role is best suited to my interests and personality that would also utilize my education, experience, and ability.

CASE PROGRESS AND CONCLUSION

Alan's therapist worked with him on the accuracy of his perception of the activating event. In reference to the examples Alan provided, his contention is that other people are not often enough being fair with him. The approach that Alan's therapist took with the systematic written homework technique was to assume that this was true and to demonstrate to Alan that it would still be irrational to demand (versus prefer) that other people be any other way. However, is it really true that other people are not often enough being reasonable and fair with him?

As Alan reflected on his accuracy of his perception of the activating event, his therapist wanted him to participate in a group therapy experience for awhile that combined expressive-emotive-experiential Gestalt therapy with REBT. He believed that Alan would benefit from further work on getting in touch with his feelings, especially in a therapeutic confrontational group setting. Group feedback on behaviors such a rationalization, denial, entitlement, and so forth, would also be helpful.

Over time Alan gained insight into the fact that, for the most part, he was expecting more from other people than they expected from him. It is irrational to think that people "should" respond to your requests even if they are fair and reasonable. However, if your requests are unreasonable, it is even more understandable why your expectations are not being fulfilled. Although Alan was now experiencing appropriate emotions of disappointment, frustration and sadness, improving the accuracy of his perception of the activating event helped to lessen the intensity of these appropriate emotions.

Alan eventually joined a business/social club in the community. His therapist indicated that Alan might want to try to improve his relationships with previous friends, family, and ex-wives. However, it would be easier to find out if he could apply the principles of intrapersonal and interpersonal functioning with totally new acquaintances. It would also be helpful to add some new relationships to his life that were not burdened by a history of previous poor interpersonal contact.

Alan discovered that he was still somewhat of a self-centered person. He did not know if he did not want to completely change or if he could not completely change. However, the fact that he was not as unreasonable as he had been before helped with new relationships. Most importantly, his reactions when some expectations of other people were not fulfilled, were more rational and emotionally appropriate. The latter helped very much because he found that other people were then more likely to tolerate his self-centeredness and focus more on his positive traits such as his charm, humor, and interesting ideas.

Alan and his therapist also discussed at length what occupational role would be best suited to his interests and personality and would also utilize his education, experience, and ability. Although his bachelor's degree was in business management, he had experienced difficulty in managerial and supervisory roles in the past. Alan had improved his interpersonal functioning, but he was uncomfortable with an administrative leadership role within an organization or managing his own business. He did like the idea of a more specialized administrative role that might allow him more autonomy or the opportunity to work more independently.

With the help of his therapist, Alan evaluated a number of occupational roles that seemed relevant, such as management analyst, quality assurance inspector, sales representative, employer relations representative, training specialist, and so forth. He also looked for opportunities in these areas available in the industrial parts company where he was currently employed as a supply clerk, as well as in other organizations. He was eventually selected by his employer for a manufacturers' representative training program.

Chapter 8

SPINAL CORD INJURY—THE CASE OF PAUL

STATEMENT OF PROBLEM AND BACKGROUND

Paul is 22 years old, unmarried, and has no children. He lives with his parents in a large urban community. Paul has a quadriplegic disability as a result of being injured in military combat. He is also experiencing intense depression associated with his disability. Paul's father, age 46, is an automotive parts store manager; his mother, age 44, is a homemaker. Paul has a sister four years older, an elementary school teacher, and a brother six years older, a restaurant manager. They have all been very emotionally supportive of Paul.

Paul was an average student in school and obtained average scores on intelligence tests. However, he excelled in athletics, playing all the major sports. He was considered physically attractive and presented himself orally very well. He had no interest in attending college and his athletic abilities were not on the level of professional sports. Consequently, upon graduation from high school, he joined the United States Marine Corps, which had been a dream of his since he was very young. He performed well in the Marine Corps, developing excellent combat skills and also continued his interest in athletics.

After three years in the Marine Corps, Paul volunteered for a combat assignment and was seriously injured. He received a medal for taking the initiative on an attack but received a gunshot wound that shattered his spinal column. Although the physicians were able to save his life, he suffered an irreversible injury very high in the spinal cord at the level of the C5 vertebra. He is paralyzed from the neck down and is totally dependent for feeding, personal hygiene, movement, dressing, writing, driving, and so forth. Although he needs assistance with feeding, he does have nearly full eating skills. He has no difficulty in breathing. Paul received good medical treatment, but he requested that he be released before his full potential for medical and physical rehabilitation could be explored.

Paul experienced a mixture of depression and disorganization from the beginning of his injury. Initially, the depression was a good sign because it was an indication that he was not in denial of his paralysis. However, the depression has continued after his return home, and he has had recurrent suicidal thoughts. A Veteran Affairs psychiatrist informed his parents of the possibility of suicide if Paul's depression continued, and they are careful to provide monitoring as well as emotional support. He continues to receive medication for his depression, but has not been receptive to seeking therapeutic counseling.

Financially, Paul does not have to consider employment. His service-connected disability retirement pays him an income higher than the average employed four-year college graduate. He also has other benefits such as medical care, personal services assistance, commissary privileges, and so forth. His parents are content to have him stay in their home indefinitely. His father, however, has wondered if Paul might be more receptive to professional counseling if it were combined with the consideration of a meaningful vocational goal. Paul reluctantly agreed to apply for benefits through the Veterans Affairs Vocational Rehabilitation Program.

COUNSELING ASSESSMENT AND STRATEGY

A Veteran Affairs (V.A.) counseling psychologist was assigned to visit Paul and assess his potential for vocational rehabilitation. A review of Paul's medical records revealed, of course, that it would be necessary that Paul be referred to a comprehensive rehabilitation facility in order to have his full potential for medical, physical, and social rehabilitation explored prior to the most effective consideration of any vocational goal. However, the counselor sensed that Paul was not in a state of mind to consider that possibility at the present time.

In order to improve his mental health potential for vocational rehabilitation, the counselor established a therapeutic relationship with Paul to explore his thoughts and feelings. Paul was very bitter that this type of disability could have happened to him. Somehow he had believed that if he had been injured in combat, it would not be of this magnitude. He assumed he would have either been killed or experienced a lesser injury. His perception of his disability at this point was that it was worse than death. He almost wished that they had not been able to save his life.

Paul had been raised with a conservative religious orientation. He had been influenced by his conservative religious training in the way it related to his patriotic interest in the Marine Corps. However, he now doubted his religion and wondered why he ever had such a strong interest in the Marine Corps. Initially, Paul's counselor listened and conveyed back to Paul that he understood the thoughts and feelings he was expressing. This approach helped to further develop rapport with Paul and facilitate a receptiveness for more direct intervention.

Eventually, Paul's counselor suggested to him that REBT might be helpful concerning the issues with which he was struggling. Paul was now more receptive to the therapeutic process and indicated a willingness to participate. Considering Paul's average academic aptitude and achievement level, his counselor presented very basic concrete examples and illustrations of the REBT process. Utilizing assistive technology, Paul was able to do some brief reading assignments and also listened to some audiotape recordings.

Initially, Paul and his counselor dealt with the issue that Paul was damning himself for not recognizing that he could be susceptible to this type of disability. His counselor helped him to realize that, even though he "could" have known, there was no reason why he "should" have known or thought about such a possibility. The evidence is that human beings often do not think of such a possibility. Further, there are many examples of people who do think of such a possibility, but it does not alter their plans. The belief that "he should have known" will contribute to feelings of guilt and depression, which will not help him with future plans.

With the help of his therapist, Paul developed the realization that his major issues were related to three basic irrational beliefs: "This disability should not have happened to me" (core iB), "Life is worthless for me" (1st derivative), and "I can't stand living this way" (2nd derivative). Paul's personality and background suggested that he could handle a very forceful therapist style. Considering also his excellent rapport with Paul, his counselor vigorously active-directively challenged and disputed Paul's irrational beliefs. They completed several sessions in this manner with good results.

Paul's counselor suggested he put these three basic irrational beliefs into the form of systematic written homework. It would provide a written record to remind and further reinforce him about what they had accomplished. He could use a tape recorder, and the V.A. could provide clerical assistance to put the material in typed form. Because they had gone over this material a number of times in their sessions, Paul was able to learn the systematic written homework procedure relatively quickly and was able to put his material into this framework with minimal assistance. His final product is represented below.

SYSTEMATIC WRITTEN HOMEWORK—PAUL

A. Quadriplegic Disability

    1. Total paralysis from the neck down.
    2. Total dependence for feeding, personal hygiene, movement, dressing, writing, driving, etc.

rB   1. This disability is reality for me.
    2. Life will be very difficult for me with this disability.
    3. I very much don't like having this disability.

iB   1. This disability shouldn't have happened to me (Core iB).
    2. Life is worthless for me with this disability.
    3. I can't stand having this disability.

C. Emotional:

    1. Intense anger related to iB # 1.
    2. Intense depression related to iB # 1, 2, & 3.

Behavioral:

    1. Withdrawal.

D. Disputing of iB # 1: This disability shouldn't have happened to me.

    D # 1 (logical dispute) Where is the logic that this disability shouldn't have happened to me?

    cE # 1: There is no reason that this disability shouldn't have happened to me because it did happen to me. Just because I did not want it to happen does not mean that it shouldn't have happened.

    D # 2 (empirical dispute) Where is the evidence that this disability shouldn't have happened to me?

    cE # 2: There is no rule or law of the universe that says that it shouldn't have happened. The reality is that these kinds of things happen.

    D # 3 (pragmatic dispute) How will holding the belief that this disability shouldn't have happened to me help me with any future goals?

cE # 3: I will probably continue to be consumed with emotions of anger and depression and withdraw from doing anything productive or useful.

D # 4 (construction rational belief) What is an alternative belief that would better help me with any future goals?

cE # 4: This condition is reality for me. I do not like it but that will not change my condition. However, I can choose to focus on ways that I can achieve goals that are realistic and are of value to me.

eE of cE's of D's of iB # 1: intense frustration and sadness about the fact that I have this disability.

Disputing of iB # 2: Life is worthless for me with this disability.

D # 1 (logical dispute) Where is the logic that life is worthless for me with this disability?

cE # 1: This disability is a major part of my life but not my whole life. It doesn't make sense to define my whole life by a part, even though a major one.

D # 2 (empirical dispute) Where is the evidence that life is worthless for me with this disability?

cE # 2: Many things in life will be difficult for me with this disability, but there are many things that I will be able to do and enjoy in life.

D # 3 (pragmatic dispute) How will holding the belief that life is worthless for me help me with any future goals?

cE # 3: It doesn't help because it causes me to avoid thinking about any future goals.

D # 4 (construction rational belief) What is an alternative rational belief that will better help me with any future goals?

cE # 4: My disability does not define all of my life. It is major and will prevent me from doing a lot of things I would like to do. However, there are many things, some I haven't even thought about yet, that I will be able to accomplish and enjoy.

eE of cE's of D's of iB # 1: Intense sadness about the limitations created by my disability. Optimistic feelings about what I might be able to accomplish.

Disputing of iB # 3: I can't stand having this disability.

D # 1 (logical dispute) Where is the logic that I can't stand having this disability?

cE # 1: I intensely dislike having this disability, but there is no reason why I can't stand it.

D # 2 (empirical dispute) Where is the evidence that I can't stand having this disability?

cE # 2: This evidence is that I can cope with having this disability and go on with my life.

D # 3 (pragmatic dispute) How will holding the belief that I can't stand having this disability help me with any future goals?

cE # 3: It won't help because it causes me to focus too much on the disability and my limitations.

D # 4 (construction rational belief) What is an alternative belief that would better help me with any future goals?

cE # 4: I am very unhappy about the fact that I have this disability, but I can stand it. Rather than focus on the disability, I can learn to cope better with it and make constructive plans for my future life.

eE of cE's of D's of iB # 3: Intense sadness that I will have to cope with having this disability the rest of my life.

bE. Homework Assignments:

1. Because the impact of my disability confused me about some of my personal values, do some values clarification with the help of my counselor.
2. Accept referral to a V.A. comprehensive rehabilitation facility where my full rehabilitation potential in regard to medical, physical, social, and vocational factors can be assessed.
3. Follow up on the recommendations of the V.A. comprehensive rehabilitation facility in consultation with my counselor.

CASE PROGRESS AND CONCLUSION

Paul now had more rational beliefs that would better assist him in the pursuit of his goals and values. The V.A. comprehensive rehabilitation facility would help him identify alternatives in regard to more concrete goals. However, where did he now stand on his personal values? The impact of his disability had confused him about some his religious beliefs and the values that had led him to the Marine Corps.

Paul's counselor primarily helped him with exploring and reflecting on his personal views. Paul eventually decided for himself that he was comfortable, in general, with the basic values he had formulated for himself before he went into the Marine Corps. He was more realistic now in the sense that he was more aware of what can happen in life. He concluded that life is a risk and that, if he worried about all the possibilities, he might never take any risks. Now is the time to go on with his life.

The evaluation that Paul received in the comprehensive rehabilitation facility was very helpful. Some useful adjustments were made relative to his medical treatment and care. In regard to his physical rehabilitation, Paul became more skilled in the use of an electronic wheelchair and other adaptive devices, allowing him greater independence. He participated in a support group with other people with quadriplegia as well as other socialization experiences. An independent living center in his local community was contacted where he could continue these kind of experiences.

Utilizing assistive technology, Paul was given various aptitude, achievement, interest, and personality tests that would have a bearing on vocational potential. Aptitude tests confirmed his intelligence testing in high school as being in the average range. However, achievement tests indicated that he would benefit from further general educational development. The latter now had more importance because of his physical limitations. It was noted that his good oral skills and physically attractive countenance would be an asset in more socially oriented vocations.

Personality testing indicated a basically healthy individual who is socially and conservatively oriented. Interest testing reflected his background in regard to social and realistic areas with high specific scores in athletics and military activities. Recommendations suggested that because he does have a certain degree of financial independence that he consider avocational as well vocational possibilities. If his goal is to be productively involved in activities highly consistent with his values and interests, there may be more opportunities in avocational endeavors.

With the help of his counselor, Paul considered some vocational possibilities related to his interests such as managing his own business, sales representative, information representative, and so forth. He and his counselor both agreed that it would be best for Paul to concentrate on his general educational development for the present. He selected a tentative vocational goal of eventually managing his own business.

While working on a year of general educational development, Paul decided to pursue an avocational interest that capitalized on his background in athletics and the Marine Corps. He became very active with the American Legion. He very much enjoyed serving as an advisor to youth activities, particularly with groups that help youth with physical or mental disabilities engage in sports activities.

Upon completion of his year of educational development, Paul decided that, rather than continue toward a vocational goal, he would continue his volunteer work with the American Legion as well as some similar activities in his local community. He could always consider a business endeavor at a later date, having developed a lot of helpful social contacts by that time. There also might eventually be some type of employment of a liaison advisory capacity that might come out of his volunteer activities. Regardless, he was content with what he considered to be a meaningful pursuit of his interests and values.

Chapter 9

SUBSTANCE ABUSE AND ADDICTION—
THE CASE OF MICHAEL

STATEMENT OF PROBLEM AND BACKGROUND

Michael is 27 years old, unmarried and has no children. He is a drafter for a large engineering firm. He was treated for an alcohol substance abuse and addiction disorder about two years ago. His employer was very cooperative in his rehabilitation, working with him through their employee assistance program. Michael participated in therapeutic activities, was able to stop drinking, and eventually returned to his work as a drafter. However, he is concerned about some of his attitudes and personality characteristics that led to his drinking problem.

Michael is an only child, and his mother and stepfather are in their late forties. Michael was eight years old when his biological father died from a heart attack. His biological father was a construction worker, and some friends and family members considered him to have an alcohol abuse and addiction problem. Michael was ten years old when his mother remarried. His stepfather is a general maintenance mechanic for a manu-facturing industry, and his mother is a homemaker. Michael's mother, biological father, and stepfather were ambitious for him and tended to push him in school. His stepfather wanted him to graduate from a university with a bachelor's degree in engineering. Michael worked hard and was a good student in high school. However, his grades and scores on admission tests were not competitive enough for admission to a university bachelor's degree engineering curriculum.

Although Michael and his mother and stepfather were disappointed, he found that he could be accepted for an associate's degree with an emphasis in drafting at a community college. He seemed to have more of an interest and ability for drafting and mechanical drawing. Consequently, he completed a two-year associate's degree and was eventually employed by a large engineering firm. His mother and stepfather were pleased that he had a good job, but Michael sensed that they were still disappointed that he had not achieved at a higher level.

Michael began to experience problems in his personal life. He seemed to have a need for rightness, orderliness, and neatness, which was helpful to him in his drafting work. However, these characteristics interfered with some interpersonal relationships. He had several relationships over time with female friends and almost got married a couple of times. His relationships with women would eventually end because they felt he was too controlling and perfectionistic. His male friends would tend to distance themselves because of his behavior.

In order to relax and better cope with stress, Michael began to increase his consumption of alcohol. He had begun drinking alcohol when he was fifteen and had already experienced some minor behavioral difficulties. His interpersonal difficulties contributed to his eventual abuse and dependence on the substance. Initially, he did not perceive that he had a problem because he primarily drank beer. However, it began to interfere with his employment. The quality of his work deteriorated, and he began to be tardy and then occasionally absent. His employer's employee assistance program helped him to see his problem and got him involved in treatment.

Michael responded well to treatment. He was able to develop insight into his need for control and was able to make a major shift in his thinking on that issue. He found that he could totally abstain from alcohol. He participated in group therapy activities and got involved with Alcoholics Anonymous (AA). Eventually, Michael returned to his position as a drafter and considered himself a recovering alcoholic. He has continued his involvement with AA and relapse prevention activities such as exercise and relaxation techniques.

About two years after his initial treatment, Michael decided that he wanted to go for individual therapy to develop a better understanding of some of the attitudes and personality characteristics that contributed to his drinking problem. He felt that individual therapy would be helpful with relapse prevention, and he was concerned about the difficulties he had experienced with interpersonal relationships, especially with women.

When Michael originally elected to go to AA, he had a choice between AA or Rational Recovery (RR), an alternate alcoholic abstinence approach based on the principles of REBT. However, he did some reading on REBT at the time and it did not appeal to him. He was having difficulty getting in touch with his feelings, and REBT principles did not seem helpful. After group therapy experiences that helped him with the expression of his feelings, he now found himself more interested in REBT. Consequently, he selected a therapist in private practice who focused on REBT.

COUNSELING ASSESSMENT AND STRATEGY

Another reason that Michael preferred AA over RR was that he liked the spiritual focus of AA. He was concerned about whether or not his spiritual beliefs would be in conflict with REBT. He discussed his orientation to spirituality, including his religious beliefs, with his therapist for awhile, and she assured him that she did not think there would be any problem. Although it is not a focus of the approach itself, she noted that many people interested and involved in RR and/or REBT, including herself, have spiritual and religious beliefs. Their ideas are similar to his and many others involved in AA, in that they prefer to believe in the probability of a higher power versus dogmatically insist that there is a higher power.

Michael's therapist further explained that REBT is basically an approach that helps one to achieve his or her own individualized personal goals and values. She noted that when most people have difficulties, it is usually related more to their attitudes about achieving their goals and values. For example, they seem to "demand" versus "desire" that they, other people, or the world be a certain way. The empirical evidence is that they can work towards such goals, but they don't have the power to guarantee their accomplishment.

Michael was very receptive to his initial orientation to REBT and highly motivated to do some reading of literature and listening to audiotapes. While he was developing a better understanding of the REBT approach, his therapist suggested that an Adlerian life-style analysis might provide some helpful background. His resentment towards his mother, biological father, and stepfather was such that she felt the life-style analysis would better help him to see his contribution to his attitudes. The analysis would also help to better identify irrational beliefs from an REBT perspective.

The Adlerian life-style analysis helped Michael to better see how he had cooperated with his mother and biological father in accepting their perfectionistic demands. His stepfather was very similar to his biological father in regard to these perfectionistic demands. He was able to understand how his early childhood recollections selectively reflected his current attitudes. He was also able to better understand how his only-child environment had helped to create some expectations of authority and life. The life-style analysis helped him to realize that he had the ability to make an impact on attitudes that would not be helpful to him in achieving his long-term goals.

Michael's therapist noted that, as Michael had correctly concluded when he entered substance abuse treatment, his major difficulties stemmed from his need to control. He had been able to make a major shift in his thinking on this issue, which had greatly helped him to be successful in his recovery thus far. However, she suggested that perhaps in terms of the REBT model he had not made an elegant or permanent change in his thinking. She sensed that either subtly, or just beneath the level of awareness, he seemed to be allowing himself to drift back into this type of thinking. Michael was very receptive to this possibility, noting that in addiction terms it meant that he had admitted to himself his need to control but had not accepted it.

With the help of his therapist, Michael identified the activating event that most bothered him was the unfairness in life. It didn't seem fair to him that the work world was so competitive. He had worked very hard in school but didn't quite have enough ability to live up to his parents' expectations. He was beginning to understand how his compulsive personality characteristics interfered with friendships, but why couldn't he be more appreciated for his conscientious behavior? He knew he had to work on his controlling tendencies if he wanted a closer love relationship with a female but felt that it shouldn't have to be so difficult.

When Michael thought about these aspects of life, identified above, he experienced anger and depression. His therapist explained the systematic written homework assignment to him and helped him to put the activating event and his emotions into this framework. Michael was then able to identify his irrational beliefs as: "Life shouldn't be unfair" (core iB), "It is awful that life is unfair" (1st derivative), and "Life is rotten because it is unfair" (2nd derivative). After a few sessions, Michael was able to complete the SWH as represented below:

SYSTEMATIC WRITTEN HOMEWORK—MICHAEL

A. Unfairness in life.

    1. Competitiveness in the work world.

    2. Not fully appreciated for my conscientious behavior by friends.

    3. Very hard for me to develop a close love relationship with a female.

rB. 1. Life is unfair.

    2. It is bad that life is unfair.

    3. Life is very difficult because it is unfair.

iB. 1. Life shouldn't be unfair (Core iB).

    2. It is awful that life is unfair.

    3. Life is rotten because it is unfair.

C. Emotional:

    1. Intense anger related to iB # 1 & 3.

    2. Intense depression related to iB # 2 & 3.

   Behavioral:

    1. Urge towards substance abuse relapse.

D. Disputing of iB # 1: Life shouldn't be unfair.

    D # 1 (logical dispute): Where is the logic that life shouldn't be unfair?

    cE # 1: There is no reason why life shouldn't be unfair because it is unfair. I don't control the universe.

    D # 2 (empirical dispute) Where is the evidence that life shouldn't be unfair?

    cE # 2: The evidence is that there are numerous examples of unfairness in life, and it is part of life.

    D # 3 (pragmatic dispute) How will holding the belief that life is unfair help me achieve my goals?

    cE # 3: It will cause me to focus too much on the unfairness in life.

    D # 4 (construction rational belief): What is an alternative belief that would better help me achieve my goals?

    cE # 4: Life includes unfairness, and I don't have absolute control over life. It would be better for me not to focus so much on the unfairness in life.

    eE of cE's of D's of iB # 4: intense anger at the unfairness in life but not at life itself.

   Disputing of iB # 2: It is awful that life is unfair.

    D # 1 (logical dispute) Where is the logic that it is awful that life is unfair?

cE # 1: It is bad that life is unfair but that does not make it awful.

D # 2 (empirical dispute) Where is the evidence that it is awful when life is unfair?

cE # 2: The evidence is that it is very difficult and hard when life is unfair but that is not the same as awful.

D # 3 (pragmatic dispute) How will holding the belief that it is awful that life is unfair help me to achieve my goals?

cE # 3: It will interfere with my thinking of ways to contribute to more fairness in life.

D # 4 (construction rational belief) What is an alternative belief that would better help me achieve my goals?

cE # 4: It is bad that life includes unfairness. The unfairness in life makes it very hard. However, it would be more helpful for me to focus on ways that I can contribute to fairness in life.

eE of cE's of D's of iB # 4: Intense sadness about the unfairness in life but not about life.

Disputing of iB # 3: Life is rotten because it is unfair.

D # 1 (logical dispute) Where is the logic that life is rotten because it is unfair?

cE # 1: I very much don't like the unfairness in life, but there is no reason why I should condemn all life.

D # 2 (pragmatic dispute) Where is the evidence that life is rotten because it is unfair?

cE # 2: The evidence is that it is very hard and difficult when life is unfair, but that is not evidence to condemn life itself.

D # 3 (pragmatic dispute) How will holding the belief that life is rotten because it is unfair help me achieve my goals?

cE # 3: It won't, because it will contribute to my returning to substance abuse behavior, which will probably destroy my life.

D # 4 (construction rational belief) What is an alternative belief that will better help me achieve my goals?

cE # 4: I very much don't like it and find it to be very difficult and hard when life is unfair. However, there is much to appreciate in life, and it would be better for me to focus on constructive ways to achieve my goals.

eE of cE's of D's of iB # 3: Intense anger and sadness about the unfairness in life but not about life.

bE. Homework Assignments:
   1. **Learn to practice Rational-Emotive Imagery (REI).**
   2. **Re-visit the issue of control with myself and other people.**
   3. **Role play in therapeutic environment.**
   4. **Apply my learning to relationships with other people.**

CASE PROGRESS AND CONCLUSION

Michael's therapist felt that he had developed a very helpful systematic written homework format on the fairness aspect because it was on a more abstract level and could be generalized to more situations. For example, they found that he could effectively generalize his learning in regard to demands about the world to demands about other people and demands about self. She also applied REBT with Michael to each of his specific examples of unfairness in life in order to make sure he had made the connection between the general and the specific.

His therapist also introduced him to negative Rational-Emotive Imagery (REI). Michael was able to perform this technique very well. He was able to imagine his specific examples of unfairness in life and experience anger and depression. He was then able to change his anger and depression to anger and sadness about the unfairness in life but not about life. When his therapist asked him how he did that, he replied with cognitive effects similar to those identified in his systematic written homework.

Michael's therapist asked him to practice his REI for thirty days to make sure he had mastered the technique and to contribute to a more permanent change in his belief system. After Michael had completed his thirty days successfully, she encouraged him to consider utilizing this technique in related situations in the future. Michael found himself using this technique after a frustrating activating event. He soon found that it was also helpful to use REI prior to and during an activating event.

Michael and his therapist re-visited the issue of control as part of his Adlerian life-style, especially in regard to his relationships with other people. From an Adlerian perspective, she had already explained to him how he took a sensitive position on issues such as fairness, conscientiousness, orderliness, etc. She further reinforced to him how control issues were part of his life-style and an important part of his identity in his relationships with other people. However, in order to more effectively relate to other people, it would be helpful for him to view his values as "desires," "wants," and "preferences" rather than "shoulds," "oughts," and "musts."

Throughout the process, the therapist used the life-style understanding as a source of encouragement to Michael. She skillfully reframed the perfectionism and controlling tendencies in his life-style as strengths in using REBT for his self-therapy. The therapist gently reminded him that these features in his life-style "cognitive blueprint" enabled him to very naturally and effectively use the detailed structure inherent in the REBT approach. Thus, she explained that his appreciation for specificity and manageability gave him an edge over most clients in using REBT. Michael was delighted to think he had a "built-in" advantage which would help him compete in a world that he judged as quite unfair.

Michael's therapist helped him to role play with her in numerous interpersonal situations in which his control issue would be a factor. As a female therapist, she was able to provide a perspective to him that would be particularly helpful in his relationships with women. Initially, he was comfortable doing these role-play exercises only in individual therapy. However, she was eventually able to persuade him to try these exercises in a group experience specifically designed for participants to practice role playing related to issues of sensitivity to them.

The next step for Michael was to apply his learning to his relationships with other people. Six months later, Michael reported to his therapist that his friends had noted a change in him, in that he was not as demanding as he had been in the past. He noticed that they seemed to be more appreciative of his conscientious behavior. His therapist noted that now that he was not imposing his values on his friends, they were more likely to notice the positive side of his values. He was also dating a female friend who, thus far, seemed to appreciate his preference to control situations as long as he took into consideration her interests and concerns.

A final issue for Michael concerned his mother and stepfather's ambitions for him. He had considered returning to school and achieving a bachelor's degree in engineering. With his work experience and performance on the job, he had now found a university that would accept him into their program, although it would still be a competitive experience. After giving it careful consideration, Michael decided that he liked his work and his current position and did not feel it was necessary to achieve at a higher level. He would rather devote the time to cultivating effective interpersonal relationships in his personal life.

Michael observed that his mother and stepfather were disappointed about his career decision. However, he noted that they seemed to have a new sense of respect for him. They conveyed to him that they were better able to accept his decision because he very much seemed to know what he wanted to do and was comfortable with himself. Michael, indeed, was comfortable with himself and his values and more confident than ever that a chemical substance would not be necessary to maintain that feeling.

CLOSING STATEMENT

As indicated in the preface, although Doctor Albert Ellis has always employed a variety of cognitive, emotive, and behavioral techniques, this textbook has focused on what made his approach radically different from other psychotherapeutic orientations: his contribution of rational restructuring or the disputing of irrational beliefs. The disputing of irrational beliefs and their relationship to emotional and behavioral change was illustrated in a systematic written homework (SWH) framework and applied to case examples of the mental health rehabilitation of individuals with mental and physical disabilities. Mental health rehabilitation was defined as therapeutic counseling designed to facilitate the emotional development of individuals with mental and physical disabilities that enables them to lead more productive lives.

Therefore, it was suggested that the textbook should be applicable to a wide variety of disciplines involved with therapeutic counseling of people with mental and/or physical disabilities such as rehabilitation counseling, mental health counseling, pastoral counseling, school counseling, clinical social work, clinical and counseling psychology, and behavioral science oriented medical specialties (e.g., psychiatry, physiatry, and occupational medicine) and related health professions (e.g., behavioral optometry, psychiatric nursing, recreational therapy, occupational therapy, and physical therapy). Readers were encouraged to conceptualize the cases in terms of their own discipline and how they might incorporate the disputing of irrational beliefs into their own therapeutic orientation.

As Doctor Ellis noted in his 1994 revision of *Reason and Emotion in Psychotherapy* (New York: Birch Lane Press) (Carol), Rational Emotive Behavior Therapy (REBT) has come a long way since he began to practice REBT in 1955. Probably most psychotherapists in the United States and the Western world now include its methods as a large part and often a main part of their practice. Aaron Beck's Cognitive Therapy, William Glasser's Reality Therapy, Arnold Lazarus's Multimodal Therapy, Maxie Maultsby's Rational Behavior Therapy, Donald Meichenbaum's

Cognitive Behavior Modification, and other practitioners' cognitive behavior therapy all include theories and practices of REBT. Moreover, therapists who call themselves "integrative," "eclectic," or "constructivist" almost always use important aspects of REBT and related cognitive behavior therapies.

Albert Ellis noted that some forms of cognitive and behavioral therapy existed before his time but were not popular. He predicts they would have grown and developed without his formulations and teachings because these are useful treatments for emotional problems and would have evolved with the changes and improvements in human science. He believes that his main achievement was to encourage their developing sooner and more effectively than otherwise might have occurred. He notes that even various mistakes he has made in theorizing, practicing, and promulgating REBT have encouraged other creative people to effectively revise and add to his original REBT—oriented practices.

As Doctor Ellis notes in his foreword to this book, Rational Emotive Behavior Therapy has always been designed to help a multiversity of individuals, including those with severe physical, mental, and emotional handicaps and disorders. He considers my book to be an authoritative and comprehensive application of REBT counseling and psychotherapy to people with rehabilitation problems and an unusual book for anyone concerned with mental and emotional rehabilitation. My final thought is that the pioneering contributions and encouragement of Albert Ellis is primarily what has helped to make this book possible.

INDEX